100 YEARS of HOLLYWOOD

A CENTURY OF MOVIE MAGIC

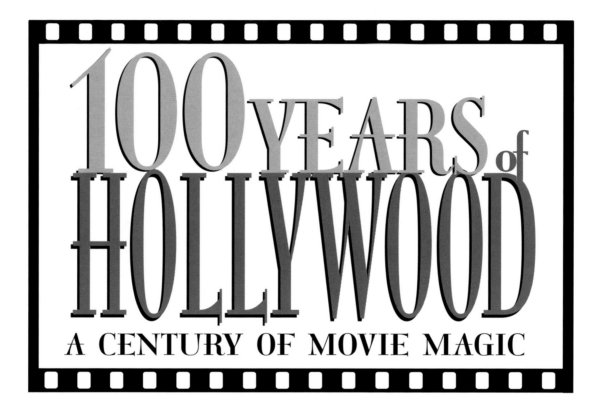

Carol Krenz

MetroBooks

MetroBooks

An Imprint of Friedman/Fairfax Publishers

Library of Congress Cataloging-in-Publication Data
Krentz, Carol.
100 years of Hollywood : a century of movie magic / Carol Krentz.
        p.   cm.
Includes bibliographical references and index.
ISBN 1-56799-645-0
1. Motion pictures—United States—History. I. Title.
PN1993.5.U6K74 1999
791.43'0973—dc21   99-36809
                                                                                      CIP

Editor: Ann Kirby
Art Director: Kevin Ullrich
Designers: Andrea Karman, Jennifer O'Connor
Photography Editor: Valerie E. Kennedy
Production Manager: Ingrid McNamara

Color separations by Fine Arts Repro. House Co., Ltd.
Printed in Hong Kong by Asia Pacific
10 9 8 7 6 5 4 3 2 1

For bulk purchases and special sales, please contact:
Friedman/Fairfax Publishers
Attention: Sales Department
15 West 26th Street
New York, NY 10010
212/685-6610 FAX 212/685-1307

Visit our website: www.metrobooks.com

Photo credits

Archive Photos: p. 88; Paramount Pictures/Fotos International: p. 45; Universal Pictures: pp. 156-157; Warner Brothers: p. 133
Camera Press/Retna Limited U.S.A.: ©E. Quinn: p. 39 **Corbis-Bettmann:** p. 126 **Corbis/Penguin:** pp. 129, 145 **Corbis/John Springer:** pp. 22,
106, 168 ©**Hulton Getty Picture Collection Limited/Tony Stone:** pp. 10, 11 top, 25, 50-51, 55 **Kobal Collection:** pp. 7 top and bottom left, 9,
18, 21, 28 left, 35, 36, 41, 42, 48, 56, 60, 62, 63, 64-65, 67, 68, 71, 76, 77, 83, 84, 87, 88, 90, 93, 97, 98, 101, 103, 105, 109, 113, 114, 119, 124-125,
127, 130, 136, 138, 140, 141, 142, 144, 148, 154, 158, 160, 162, 170 **Museum of Modern Art Film Still Archives:** pp. 11 bottom, 16-17, 19, 20,
53, 59, 94-95 **Photofest:** pp. 2, 5, 6, 7 right, 8, 13, 14, 15, 24, 27, 28 right, 31, 32-33, 40, 47, 52, 72, 78-79, 80, 91, 102, 110, 118, 121, 122, 135,
146, 149, 150, 152, 153, 159, 164-165, 166 **Retna Limited U.S.A.:** ©Holland: p. 108 **Stills/Retna Limited U.S.A.:** pp. 75, 117

Page 2: Boris Karloff brought Frankenstein's monster to life in the 1931 horror classic, and made himself a star in the process.
Page 5: Cary Grant in *North by Northwest* (1959). Page 6: Buster Keaton, the "great stone face" of the silent era.

Dedication

Jiminy Cricket and Walt Disney were the first to teach me that imagination makes wishes come true. This book is for them—and for everyone who has ever believed in the power of magic.

Acknowledgments

I wish to thank Faye Weber for her unwavering support and encouragement—it made all the difference; Gabriella Adler for her keen insight and comments, Gary Krenz for his suggestions and generous assistance with research, the librarians at the Westmount Public Library, Westmount, Quebec, for their incredible patience, the entire staff at Club Video Centre, Montreal, who provided me with much-needed reference materials, and my editor at Michael Friedman, Ann Kirby, who wrestled this book to the ground. I'd also like to thank photo editor Valerie Kennedy for her careful selections and Jennifer O'Connor and Andrea Karman, who handled the book's design. I especially want to thank my husband Gilbert Sureau for countless selfless weekends when his soup and sandwiches got me through another ten pages.

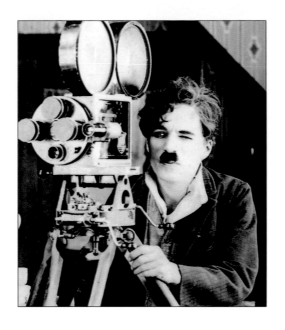

Contents

....

HOLLYWOOD
and the
Twentieth Century

The turn of the twentieth century in the United States was a time of great change and social upheaval. Vast numbers of immigrants arrived on American shores seeking to make their names in a place where it was rumored the streets were paved with gold.

It was also a time of revolutionary inventions, most significantly—for our purposes—the birth of motion pictures. Movies as we know them today are the result of the efforts of many inventors and experimenters who toyed with the idea of capturing motion on film for a variety of reasons. Some were concerned with profit, others with art; some specialized in technology, others in biology.

The first "movie" was made to settle a bet. In 1872, Leland Stanford, former governor of California, bet a friend that when a horse gallops, all four of its feet leave the ground at one point. He commissioned photographer Eadweard Muybridge to help prove his theory.

After five years of experimentation, Muybridge finally succeeded in doing so. He strung a series of lines across a racetrack and attached them to the shutters on a series of cameras. When a horse was sent down the track, the animal broke the strings as it came across them; the horse's legs (yes, they all left the ground) were captured in a series of twenty-four consecutive still photographs. Although this galloping horse experiment was performed with still photos, it was the running of these photos consecutively that was pivotal to the future of motion pictures. Also, this experiment spurred Muybridge to invent the earliest projector, the zoopraxiscope, a machine that could project images in large format onto a screen from a motion wheel.

Muybridge wasn't alone in his experiments. Overseas in France, inventor Jules Étienne Marey developed the first motion picture camera in the late 1880s, and in 1892, the first projector to use celluloid film on an endless belt.

Inventor Thomas Alva Edison met Muybridge in the late 1880s to examine the zoopraxiscope. Edison also studied the work of Marey, whose motion picture projector he improved upon by perforating the film at regular intervals so that it could be held on the camera. Edison added this enhancement to his own invention, the kinetoscope, a machine that actually displayed ninety-second motion pictures. The kinetoscope placed him at the forefront of the industry, as it was the first

commercial motion picture machine. Edison didn't bother to patent his invention; instead, he quickly set up a distribution network and made a fast and hefty profit selling his machines across the United States.

Movie technology continued to grow by leaps and bounds throughout the end of the nineteenth century. French brothers Auguste and Louis Lumière created the cinématographe, a cheaper, less cumbersome machine than Edison's. Because the portable cinématographe made it possible to film moving pictures just about anywhere and show them to a large crowd of paying customers, it proved very profitable. Edison retaliated with a similar projector, the Vitascope, in 1896.

As the kinetoscope gave way to the film projector, entrepreneurs quickly set about finding venues in which to show movies. Vaudeville theaters strung twelve-minute films together and showed them as grand finales to live stage productions. Unfortunately, it was the popularity of film that lead to Vaudeville's eventual demise.

Even though the films were a big hit, audiences were limited. Most patrons of vaudeville were white-collar men and women who had an entire quarter—big money in those days—to spend on a show. The less fortunate had to do without. It quickly occurred to many theater owners and

Page 8: David O. Selznick cut his producing teeth at RKO with the classic adventure/fable, *King Kong* (1933), starring Fay Wray.

Page 9: British director David Lean's *Doctor Zhivago* (1965), was a critical and financial success.

Above: Eadweard Muybridge's stills of the galloping horse that formed the prototype of the first motion picture.

Left: Thomas Edison and his kinetoscope, which he presented at the 1893 Chicago World's Columbian Exposition.

businessmen that there was a great deal of money just waiting to be made if more people had access to the movies. Penny arcade owners began to set up movies for a nickel in their establishments. These movies became so popular that businessmen turned arcades and vacant stores into theaters called nicolets, nickeldromes, and eventually, nickelodeons. In most cases, the nickelodeons weren't very clean, and the movies of the day were slightly prurient. Mixed in with assorted boxing matches, crashing locomotives, and silly comedy sketches were bawdy burlesque films.

The advent of feature films gave birth to the first movie palaces. The Art Nouveau and Art Deco movements served as inspirational backdrops for the new plush theaters, which sprang up in the 1920s. Carpeted, opulent, and comfortable, these theaters seated up to 2,000 people. In New York, these palaces included the Strand, Rialto, Rivoli, Roxy, and Radio City Music Hall. In Hollywood, there was, most notably, Sid Grauman's Chinese Theater (now Mann's Chinese Theater, where the hand- and footprints of movie stars are immortalized in cement, along with their autographs).

In the years following World War I, the world was changing. New freedoms and ideas bubbled to the surface, bringing with them revolutionary expressions and directions in art, poetry, music, theater, and literature. In this environment, the new movie moguls thrived.

Initially based in New York, these first film giants moved to California and established Hollywood in Los Angeles, where real estate was cheap and plentiful, and warm, dry,

and predictable weather conditions enabled pioneer filmmakers to shoot continuously throughout the year. Additionally, southern California was largely undeveloped at the time, and the region around Hollywood offered exotic foliage, glacial mountain peaks, and desert tumbleweeds all within a relatively small area.

In 1923, producer-director Mack Sennett, Harry Chandler, and the *Los Angeles Times* chipped in to erect a landmark sign that read "Hollywoodland" to attract land developers and investors—which no doubt it did. But more importantly, for the mere price of $21,000, it spelled out one of the most significant American discoveries. The sign, which would later be shortened to Hollywood, came to embody fame, glamour, and dizzying power—the very epitome of movie magic.

The years following the 1929 Wall Street stock market crash were turbulent ones for Americans, but against this pessimistic backdrop, Hollywood somehow thrived. As Americans struggled with the indignity of bread lines, they looked to the power of the big screen and were willing to do just about anything to scrape up the necessary dimes needed for an escape.

Hollywood returned the favor by serving up the most hilarious, stirring, poignant, daring, sweeping, and inspirational material ever to appear on its menu during the 1930s. Even today, as we examine the decades that followed, no other time in motion picture history quite compares. In 1938, 769 movies were released and 80 million movie tickets were sold every week, which means that about 65 percent of the U.S. population went to the movies regularly; in 1994,

approximately 470 movies were released and only 25 million tickets were sold weekly, meaning that less than 10 percent of the population paid to see first-run films.

By the early 1940s, Hollywood had become distracted by World War II, and mainstream storytelling evolved to incorporate wide-ranging emotions and conflicts. Movies became the eye on world events. Great documentaries poured forth, outlining Hitler's military strategies and the Allied Forces' struggles. Movies were rallying, patriotic calls to service, country, and honor, as well as the vehicles for wartime romances, propaganda, homespun hero stories, religious revelations, musical escapades, and ultimately, dark and sinister depictions of emotional terrors within the American people. Filmmakers like Alfred Hitchcock added greater dimensions in terror, suggesting that evil could exist anywhere and strike anyone, even in the most innocent of places.

Above: The world-famous, $21,000 "Hollywoodland" sign, erected to attract real estate developers in 1923. Over the years, through many renovations, the landmark has become the legendary symbol of the Hollywood dream. In 1932, a failed starlet jumped to her death from the "H."

It was by and large a decade of personal angst. The movies reflected the American sense of desperation. Murmurs of Communist infiltration began and the seeds of the McCarthy era were planted. Hollywood's Golden Age was about to draw its last breath.

In the 1950s, the United States enjoyed a postwar boom, but Hollywood's role was more reactionary than visionary. Studio heads waged war against television, rather than harnessing the new medium's potential. When it was clear that the bulk of the American population had essentially moved to the suburbs, Hollywood did not rush to invest in suburban theaters, missing its chance to capitalize on the new American middle class. Instead of frolicking in the exhilarating waters of the United States' postwar prosperity, Hollywood almost drowned.

The House Un-American Activities Committee (HUAC) further weakened Hollywood's popularity in the 1950s. Those fingered in the industry had but two choices: admit to Communist sympathies and offer names of those they'd fraternized with to avoid going to jail, or take the Fifth Amendment, which kept them out of jail but placed them on the infamous blacklist. Great talent died in Hollywood as a result. Many blacklisted writers worked under pseudonyms to stay alive until the 1960s.

Television eventually showed itself as a threat to the movie industry, and the attempts to fight it were numerous, if ill conceived. Until 1956, no Hollywood film could be shown on television, and Hollywood actors and actresses were forbidden to appear in a television program. This left the door open for non-Hollywood actors to win the hearts of the American public as they made big names for themselves on the small screen. The growing popularity of television led the great sumptuous movie palaces—no longer supported by the major studios—to suffer diminished audiences and enormous losses. One by one, these theaters turned into gas stations, shopping malls, apartment houses—even parking lots.

By the 1960s, Hollywood was on the decline, but because it was so adept at putting on a great show, few outsiders noticed. Movie stars, their entourages, and gossip machines continued to hold pride of place in the entertainment

Above: When the House Un-American Activities Committee began its second reign of terror in Hollywood, it was met with some talented resistance, including Richard Conte, June Havoc, John Huston, Humphrey Bogart, Lauren Bacall, Joe Sistrom, Evelyn Keyes, Danny Kaye, John Shepherd, and Jane Wyatt.

Opposite: Blonde bombshell Jean Harlow adds her footprints to the Walk of Fame outside Grauman's Chinese Theater.

magazines and on late-night television. And movies were still coming out of Hollywood—but there were increasingly fewer of them. Television proved that its power was supreme, especially when it came to covering world-shaking events. The first televised presidential debates, the assassination of President Kennedy, the horrors of the Vietnam War—all could be seen in the privacy of one's own living room. And as audience demand for entertainment in the form of movies lessened, studio revenues fell.

Fortunately, Hollywood experienced a renaissance in the first part of the 1970s. Innovations and influences came from

independent and radical filmmakers, European styles of cinema, and the accumulated pent-up frustrations of the younger generation. The 1970s saw the birth of the mega-blockbuster. And the way movies were publicized and distributed during this decade laid the groundwork for the next wave of independents in the late 1980s and 1990s.

The Hollywood of the 1980s had more than just television to compete with. New technologies, such as video games and VCRs, had begun to surface and make their way into American homes. Not wishing to repeat its mistakes of the 1950s, the new "hip" Hollywood wholeheartedly embraced the latest media developments. Films such as *Star Wars* had embraced new technologies and sparked the age of the blockbuster in the previous decade, and in the 1980s,

Hollywood furthered the trend, producing additional box-office phenomena and setting the stage for spin-off merchandising. Even the most celebrated artistic efforts of the decade, such as *Gandhi* and *Out of Africa*, were larger-than-life productions with huge budgets.

As the last decade of the century dawned, new contenders for Hollywood's prized status presented themselves. The home computer became as ubiquitous as the refrigerator. Global access to entertainment was gained through the information superhighway. Hollywood drastically increased its output to fill all the new available venues for its product. Television stars crossed over into films. Movies bypassed theaters and went straight to video. Films were based on successful television shows and even video games—and the other way around. Remakes and sequels abounded.

Yet despite the trend toward big-budget, money-making films, the 1990s have also provided surprisingly fertile ground for a new generation of independent filmmakers, enabling smaller films like *Clerks* (1994) to become breakout hits.

A complete history of Hollywood would no doubt fill a bookshelf of its own, or at least act as a pretty impressive doorstop. This book instead presents a sampling of all that Hollywood has given to us during the past century. What you will find within these pages is a tribute to just some of the greats, from the first movie moguls to the most controversial directors to the brightest stars. So butter your popcorn, sit back in your seat, and wait for the curtain to go up on your tour of one hundred years of movie magic.

MOGULS
AND
MASTERMINDS

I n the beginning, there were no limits to what filmmakers could put on movie screens. However, these early freedoms were short-lived. Eventually, the clergy, the press, and law enforcement deemed the content of movies evil and the nickelodeons that showed them an abomination, so a shutdown of all nickelodeons was ordered and licenses were revoked. The new regime raised license fees, placed theaters under police jurisdiction rather than licensing bureaus, and began restricting the attendance of children.

Before the crackdown, Thomas Edison had organized the Motion Pictures Patents Company (MPPC), a huge trust that controlled every aspect of the movie industry, keeping his own company, Biograph, at the helm. The MPPC won the favor of the newly emerged controlling powers because it created a self-regulatory body to act as a censor. Film producers agreed to submit all films to the New York Board of Censorship (later called the National Board of Review of Motion Pictures), which would examine all films and remove all obscenities. Edison's trust flourished, but others were furious at the monopoly and were determined to break it up.

Independent filmmakers fought back. Because the MPPC thought them too weak to worry about, it made the mistake of ignoring them. In 1912, the government got involved and quickly filed suit against the trust, charging it with violating the 1890 antitrust laws. Finally, by 1915, Edison's trust was dissolved, creating the opportunity for the first film moguls to come to power. These men would shape Hollywood's future.

The First GIANTS

independents soon followed suit. Laemmle attacked MPPC with ads he ran in trade publications and gained the support of exhibitors by not charging weekly license fees.

In 1910, Laemmle organized a slew of independents into a company called Motion Picture Distributing and Sales, and later, the Universal Film Manufacturing Company. He established the Universal Film Company with Patrick Power in 1912 and opened Universal City in California in 1915.

Joining the crusade was William Fox, a tenacious entrepreneur who broke through by building larger, more comfortable movie theaters. Flush with success, he decided to become a distributor. The MPPC tried to buy him out, and when he resisted, it revoked his license. Rather than succumb to defeat, Fox pioneered new directions in the industry by becoming a producer, distributor, and exhibitor under the dome of one company. In 1915, he created the Fox Film Corporation.

Among the first independents to wage war against the MPPC was "Uncle" Carl Laemmle, referred to as such because he gave jobs to everyone in his family—and anyone else who impressed him in any way. Everyone was drawn to Uncle Carl.

Laemmle personally pioneered the star system. Biograph and the MPPC never gave their feature players any billing, afraid that doing so might encourage them to ask for bigger salaries. So Laemmle wooed actresses such as Mary Pickford with better deals and star billing, using their popularity to draw audiences. Word quickly got out. "Stars" were boosting sales better than any other method of advertising, and other

Pages 16-17: German director Fritz Lang's silent-film masterpiece *Metropolis* (1926) is a compelling story about a futuristic city and a mechanized society.

Page 18: Darryl F. Zanuck and Twentieth Century Fox Pictures brought John Steinbeck's *The Grapes of Wrath* to the screen in 1940. Directed by John Ford, the film provided actor Henry Fonda with the greatest role of his career.

Page 19: Cinematographer G.W. (Billy) Bitzer (left) and director D.W. Griffith (right) changed the course of filmmaking, notably with *The Birth of a Nation* (1915) and *Intolerance* (1916).

Above: Elfin producer "Uncle" Carl Laemmle was one of the first studio giants, founding the Universal Film Company in 1912. Opposite: The assassination of Abraham Lincoln by John Wilkes Booth at Ford's Theater in D.W. Griffith's epic, *The Birth of a Nation*.

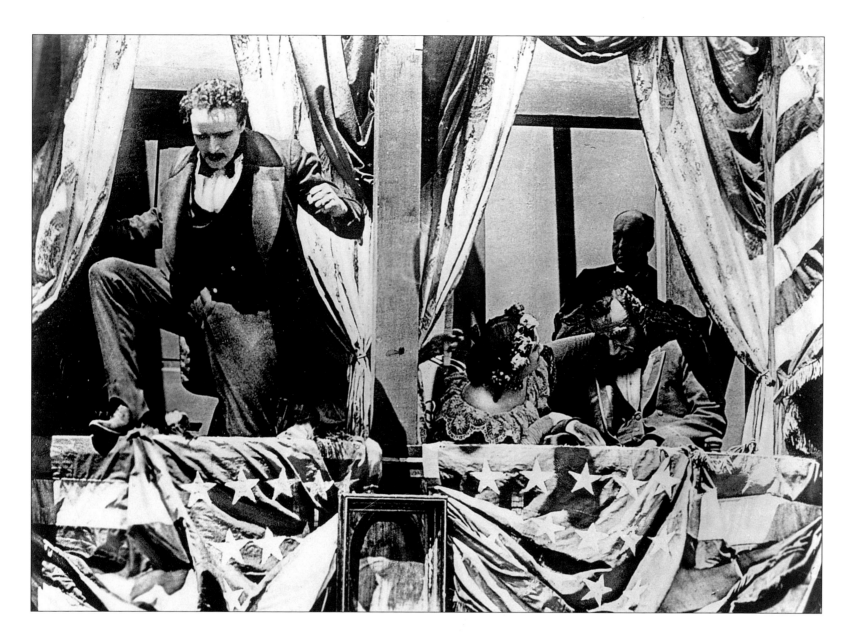

Artistic films made Fox's early reputation and spurred his rise to fame, and he received the first and only Academy Award for Artistic Quality of Production in 1927 for the film *Sunrise*. Like Laemmle, Fox used the publicity machine to create movie stars. He also pioneered the newsreel with the creation of Fox Movietone News in 1927.

But Fox began a fall from grace in the 1920s. He conspired with Loew's head Nicholas Schenck to acquire ownership of the Loew's theaters, hoping the move would mean a merger with Metro-Goldwyn-Mayer that would ultimately eliminate Paramount, Fox's major rival. But Fox's financial situation was not stable as the stock market crash approached, and didn't have as much influence in politics as he had thought— or as much as his rival Louis B. Mayer—and his plans for a merger blew up in his face. In 1935, his production company merged with Darryl F. Zanuck's Twentieth Century Productions to become Twentieth Century Fox, but by 1936 Fox had declared bankruptcy.

Louis B. Mayer worked in his father's ship-salvaging business until he bought a theater in 1907 in Haverhill, Massachusetts, where he showed motion pictures. His first big success as a film distributor was *The Birth of a Nation* (1915). In 1918, he established Louis B. Mayer Studios in Los Angeles.

In the 1920s, theater giant Marcus Loew bought two struggling companies, Metro Pictures and Goldwyn Pictures, and placed Louis B. Mayer in charge. The new company was called Metro-Goldwyn-Mayer, or MGM. Mayer, more a bean counter than an illusionist, had the wisdom to recognize talent when he saw it. He put the young Irving Thalberg in charge of day-to-day movie production, giving him the added

Above: History in the making as singer Al Jolson breaks the silence barrier in the Warner Brothers film *The Jazz Singer* (1927). Charlie Chaplin mourned the loss of silent films, stating that "Motion pictures need dialogue as much as Beethoven symphonies need lyrics."

responsibility of approving all film projects for MGM. In addition to the genius of Thalberg was the backing the Loew's corporation—and its hundreds of prime theaters across the United States. MGM set up studios on Samuel Goldwyn's former lot in Culver City, California.

In 1916, Adolph Zukor, a onetime partner of Marcus Loew, bought Jesse Lasky's Feature Play company to create Famous Players-Lasky. Zukor also absorbed the Lewis J. Selznick Picture Co., Edwin S. Porter's Rex Pictures, Pallas Pictures, and Morosco Pictures. A distribution company, Paramount Pictures, was added as well, and this was the name chosen to represent the entire empire. During the era of silent films, Paramount Pictures became the most powerful studio.

Zukor had enormous capital to invest in the form of huge salaries for its star players. After actors finished stints at Universal or Biograph, they flocked to Paramount for lucrative contracts. The "A, B, C" film category system was born through Zukor at Paramount. An "A" picture, which usually captured a stage production on film, was considered the highest standard in taste and intellectual pursuit. However, public preferences soon turned to the more mainstream "B" movies. Over the years, "B" movies were elevated to "A" status and "C's" became the cheap "B" pictures, the second halves of the double-bills.

Heading Paramount, Zukor faced repeated crises, losses of revenue, and hostile power struggles from within and without. He led the industry through the silent years but was caught unprepared by talking films.

Warner Bros. (formed by Warner brothers Albert, Harry, Sam, and Jack), on the other hand, flourished when sound became a reality in motion pictures. Established in 1919, it was a quiet studio with almost no chance of longevity save for one important risk-taking decision—it was the first to invest in sound. In 1925, Warner Bros. bought Vitagraph and its sound technology. Al Jolson's voice in *The Jazz Singer* (1927) catapulted them into prominence.

The back-stabbing and viciousness that unfailingly illustrates the business ethics of Hollywood was best expressed by one of the more likable moguls, Samuel Goldwyn, who said, "In this business it's dog eat dog and nobody's going to eat me." Tired of partners and iffy companies, Goldwyn decided to strike out on his own. Samuel Goldwyn, Inc. was founded in 1924, dedicated to films of stature and important themes, suitable for all family members.

Latecomers Harry and Jack Cohn, along with Joe Brandt, formed Columbia Pictures in 1924. Their rise was not due to groundbreaking film innovation but rather to an innovative director, Frank Capra.

Radio-Keith-Orpheum (RKO) was founded in 1928. It produced a few memorable films, most notably Orson Welles's *Citizen Kane* (1941), but RKO's run was brief. The studio went into receivership in 1933. It limped along, eventually sinking into bankruptcy in the early 1950s when it was taken over by Irving Trust, who divided it among RCA, Time Inc., Rockefeller Center, and Atlas Corporation. In 1953, the studios were taken over by Desilu Productions.

Visionaries

Starting around the 1920s, it was becoming apparent to the industry that the role of producer and director must be split into separate functions in order to accommodate the ever-increasing demand for films. For a while, the director was a mere link in a chain of command, with little artistic control. But times changed. Directors have truly played an integral role in making Hollywood the powerful force it has become.

The Pioneers

....

The evolution of the new studio system can be traced back to Thomas H. Ince, whose uncanny sense of great moviemaking vaulted him into the silent era with considerable notice. Save for one major film, *Civilization* (1916), seen largely as an antiwar epic that reflected Woodrow Wilson's foreign policies, Ince told sweeping stories filled with cinematic effects, such as dust and smoke swirling through the scenery.

Also a pioneer, D.W. Griffith was the flash point through which a torrent of modern films and art sprang. He began his career as an actor in local productions and soon started to write plays. He sold one-reel scenarios first to Edwin S. Porter and then to Biograph Pictures. When Biograph had an opening for a director in 1908, he was hired. Over the next five years his output was enormous—some 400 films, most of them twelve minutes in length.

While at Biograph, Griffith either introduced or perfected the techniques of motion-picture pageantry: the close-up, the scenic long shot or panoramic view, and cross-cutting— the process of editing different scenes together and intermixing them to give the audience the impression that separate events are occurring simultaneously.

Unhappy with the short length of Biograph's films, Griffith moved to Mutual Films with the understanding that he could mount larger, more ambitious projects as a director and supervisor. His method of intercutting scenes with parallel story lines confounded most film producers. They thought his narratives difficult and insisted they were far too complicated for movie audiences. Griffith countered by saying that if audiences could follow Charles Dickens, they could surely follow his movies.

Griffith's two most important works, *The Birth of a Nation* (1915) and *Intolerance* (1916) are still well respected and have become the source of inspiration for generations of filmmakers. Griffith made several more films, but as the years

Page 24: Director Cecil B. DeMille's biblical epic *The Ten Commandments* was a box office hit both in 1923 (shown here) and again in 1956. A showman in the Barnum & Bailey tradition, DeMille perfected the art of the spectacle.

Page 25: The quintessential authority of suspense and horror, Alfred Hitchcock wove sardonic humor into the gruesome and the mysterious.

Opposite: "America's Sweetheart" Mary Pickford was as brilliant at business as she was in acting. Pickford formed United Artist with husband Douglas Fairbanks, Charlie Chaplin, and D.W. Griffith in 1919.

Above: Director Cecil B. DeMille, seated in front of a poster for *The Squaw Man* (1914) — his first motion picture, and the first feature-length film made in Hollywood.

Above: Zazu Pitts (left) and Gibson Gowland (right) star in director Erich Von Stroheim's masterpiece, *Greed* (1924). Supposedly, producer Irving Thalberg cut *Greed's* running time from its original three hours to 140 minutes; yet, in its present form, *Greed* remains a feat of genius.

Moguls
and
Masterminds

moved forward, he lapsed into a downward spiral. He helped form United Artists with Charlie Chaplin, Mary Pickford, and Douglas Fairbanks in 1919, but his own company began to flounder owing to bad pictures and the vagaries of the economy of the 1920s. He was bought out in 1933.

A former actor, Cecil B. DeMille produced lavish spectacles with broad strokes and hocus-pocus theatricals. He believed he was giving audiences what they wanted, and in so doing, he conjured up grandiose morality films with plenty of spice and sex and ultimate retribution. DeMille found his true niche in

biblical epics such as *The Ten Commandments*, which he made in 1923 and again in 1956. These and other large narratives, such as *The Greatest Show on Earth* (1952), allowed ample room for storytelling, while at the same time providing larger-than-life locales and casts of thousands.

Whereas DeMille gave the people what they wanted, director Erich von Stroheim's concern lay in giving the audience what he wanted them to have. In such films as *Foolish Wives* (1922) and *Greed* (1925) his subject matter included the ugly, the cruel, and the grotesque, suggesting that life was a smooth, rather inane flat rock straddling vermin and darkness beneath. Stroheim was greatly influenced technically by D.W. Griffith, but his subject matter and his impossible meticulousness over every frame of his films were all his own.

At twenty years old, Irving Thalberg, "the boy wonder of Hollywood" headed up production at MGM while he was too young to sign the checks! He started off working for Carl Laemmle at Universal. When he got a little too big for Laemmle's fragile ego, he left and went to MGM where he stayed for fourteen years with Louis B. Mayer's paternal blessing. Mayer liked to encourage his stars; Thalberg had sympathy for the writers. Thalberg spent almost every waking hour in projection rooms, story meetings, and readings, all the while struggling with a heart condition. His personal talent lay in film editing, and his grasp of movie magic was unrivaled. Ambitious, driven, critical yet polished, and aristocratic by nature, Thalberg ensured that other talents thrived.

Thalberg backed Tod Browning's *Freaks* (1932), a sideshow exposé of human oddities including dwarfs, a human torso, and various other carnival monstrosities. Louis B. Mayer, Thalberg's employer, was outraged at the film's premiere. The movie was unique to be sure, but so grotesque it was pulled out of circulation, cut, then reissued. That didn't stop England from banning the film for thirty years. Upon its re-release the title was changed to *Nature's Mistakes*. Some of Thalberg's other memorable productions include *Mutiny on the Bounty* (1935), *Romeo and Juliet* (1936), *The Good Earth* (1937), and *Marie Antoinette* (1938). Unfortunately, Thalberg

did not get to see the finished versions of his last two films, as he died in September 1936 at the age of thirty-seven.

Like those of DeMille, producer David O. Selznick's films were lavish and epic. At the same time, they were tightly focused, well written, and thoroughly developed. He proved himself at RKO and delivered such films as *A Bill of Divorcement* (1932), which launched Katharine Hepburn's career, *King Kong* (1933), and *Little Women* (1933), which also starred Katharine Hepburn. He soon joined his father-in-law, Louis B. Mayer, at MGM, where he produced among others, *Dinner at Eight* (1933), *Viva Villa!* (1934), and *Manhattan Melodrama* (1934), which introduced Mickey Rooney to audiences. Three very successful films emerged next: *David Copperfield, A Tale of Two Cities,* and *Anna Karenina*—all in 1935.

Hot-tempered and ambitious, Selznick wanted out of MGM. Mayer tried to dissuade him but to no avail. In 1935, Selznick International was launched—its first film was *Little Lord Fauntleroy* (1936). Next came *The Garden of Allah* (1936), in Technicolor, starring Marlene Dietrich. Another color experimentation was *A Star Is Born* (1937). Selznick also produced *Nothing Sacred* (1937), and his most important film, *Gone With the Wind* (1939), starring Clark Gable and the vivacious Vivien Leigh. In 1940, he worked his magic again with novelist Daphne du Maurier's haunting tale *Rebecca*, starring Laurence Olivier and Joan Fontaine.

Selznick's career took a downward spiral when he fell in love with and married actress Jennifer Jones and placed her at the top of his list of priorities. Obsessive about most things in his life, he was consumed with Jones's wardrobe, her camera angles, and her persona, and eventually was unable to see the forest for the trees. After a long series of pictures that fell short of the stature of his earlier achievements, he took a ten-year leave of absence. He died of a heart attack in 1965 before he had a chance to make a comeback.

Another film pioneer, Darryl Zanuck, headed in the 1920s to California, where he was able to sell a few short pieces of writing. He broke into films at Warner Bros., becoming a staff writer and penning the plots for most of the *Rin Tin Tin* movies. His scripts were terrible but his enthusiasm was contagious. He became studio manager and Jack Warner's right hand by 1928—but the stint was short lived. In 1933, after much disagreement and wrangling, Zanuck struck out on his own and formed a small company, Twentieth Century Pictures, with backing from Joseph Schenck, brother of Nicholas Schenck, head of Loew's Inc.

The Shirley Temple phenomenon was Zanuck's gift to the industry. Signing a mere child of four to a contract may have seemed crazy to outside observers, but little Shirley Temple's bright eyes, golden ringlets, and happy toe-stepping filled the studio's coffers, with such successes as *Dimples* (1936), *Heidi* (1937), and *Rebecca of Sunnybrook Farm* (1938). Among Zanuck's most famous films are *Laura* (1944) and *All About Eve* (1950).

During the gradual demise of the studio system in the late 1950s and 1960s, Zanuck breathed new life into Twentieth

Century Fox with *The Longest Day* (1962), *Cleopatra* (1963), *The Sound of Music* (1965), *MASH* (1970), and *Patton* (1970).

Golden Boys of the Golden Age

A new wave of directors came about in the 1920s and 1930s, bringing new visions to the big screen. George Cukor was a distinguished stage director in the 1920s before he made his pilgrimage to Hollywood in 1929. He signed on with Paramount and made his directorial debut with *Tarnished Lady* in 1931. He was hired by David O. Selznick to direct *A Bill of Divorcement* (1932), the film that sparked Cukor's lifelong friendship with Katharine Hepburn. When Selznick moved to MGM shortly afterward, he took Cukor with him. There, Cukor flourished with *Camille* (1937) and *Holiday* (1938), working again with Hepburn on the latter. The original director of *Gone With the Wind* (1939), Cukor was fired on account of irreconcilable differences with Clark Gable.

Cukor teamed up again with Hepburn and Cary Grant—and Jimmy Stewart—to make *The Philadelphia Story* (1940) and went on to direct Hepburn and Spencer Tracy in *Adam's Rib* (1949) and *Pat and Mike* (1952). In 1964, he won his only Academy Award, for *My Fair Lady*.

Opposite: Vivien Leigh proved that she was the definitive Scarlett O'Hara both onscreen and off. When she received a one-pound memo from the obsessive memo-writing Selznick, she not only read it through, but answered it point by excruciating point. It took her ten days.

John Ford made his biggest splash in westerns, but he wasn't limited to that genre. *The Iron Horse* (1924) hinted at the directorial prowess that was to come. He made *The Informer* in 1935, which garnered him a Best Director Oscar. In 1939, three of Ford's films were released, one of which was *Stagecoach*, the film that made Ford legendary and John Wayne a star. In the early 1940s, Ford won consecutive Oscars for *The Grapes of Wrath* (1940) and *How Green Was My Valley* (1941). He went on to make many more films from the 1940s through the 1960s, several starring Wayne.

With thrillers such as *Scarface* (1932), and classic screwball comedies such as *Twentieth Century* (1934), *Bringing Up Baby* (1938), and *His Girl Friday* (1940), Howard Hawks won audiences with his clean visual style and fast-talking characters. He paired Humphrey Bogart with newcomer Lauren Bacall in *To Have and Have Not* (1944) and *The Big Sleep* (1946), and discovered Marilyn Monroe, giving her roles in *Monkey Business* (1952) and *Gentlemen Prefer Blondes* (1953). Although he never won an Oscar for a specific film, he was awarded an honorary Oscar in 1974.

Right: Chock-full of wide-eyed idealism, Jimmy Stewart's Mr. Smith arrives in Washington in Frank Capra's 1939 classic film. Stewart, who earned an Academy Award nomination for the role, summed up his acting technique this way: "I don't act. I react."

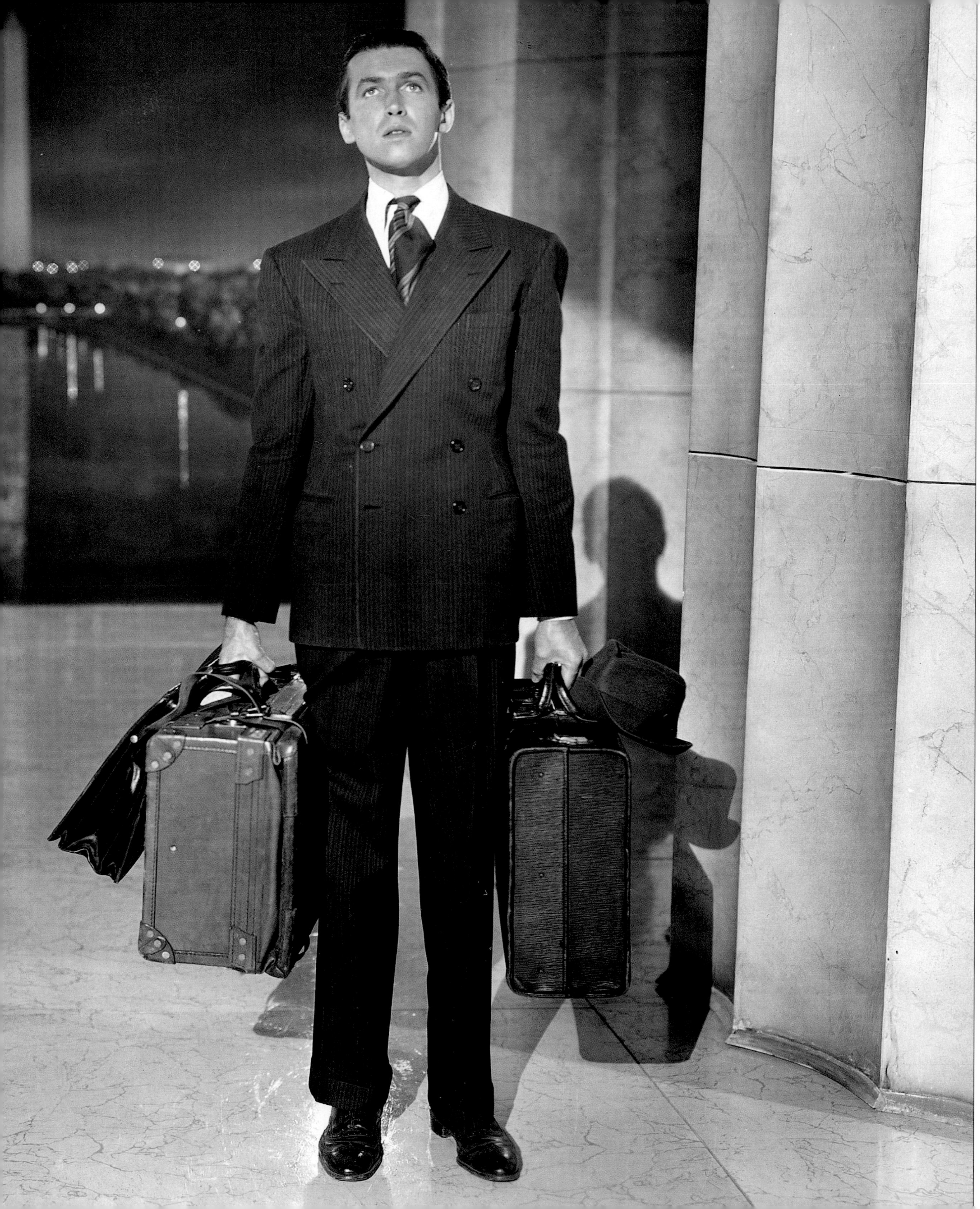

Magicians of Life and Art

Other talents emerged during Hollywood's Golden Age, lending their own brand of magic to audiences in theaters across the United States. Animator Walt Disney found a way to harness mass culture and shape it. Walt Disney Pictures grew out of companies formed in the 1920s and was incorporated in 1929. Thanks to Disney's singular vision, the company thrived and continued to expand, becoming one of the world's largest corporations.

Before audiences' eyes, Disney and his animators rapidly grew in technical sophistication. Their artwork became more integrated and complex while their subject matter ventured, at times, into the macabre, as in *The Silly Symphony* (1929). But shortly after Disney embarked upon these forays into the creatively bizarre, the Breen Office's enforcement of the 1930 Hollywood Production Code (which had been largely unenforced from 1930 until Joseph I. Breen took over at the Production Code Administration in 1934) began to have an influence. Disney was no longer permitted to draw comical cows with jiggling udders, for example—in fact, no udders were allowed at all.

Disney's *Snow White and the Seven Dwarfs* (1937) was the first full-length animated film. Since then, Walt Disney Studios has consistently produced classics that sweep their share of accolades. Today, Disney's original characters remain American icons.

Frank Capra didn't use animation in his films, but he conjured another kind of magic through them. He managed to tap into the human heart in such a way as to unify the United States in one determined vision. Capra's films, although sometimes bleak, nevertheless satisfied the conscience, fed the soul of America in the Depression years, and offered a sense of hope.

Capra's move to romantic comedy in *It Happened One Night* (1934), starring Claudette Colbert and Clark Gable, made all the difference in his career. It won the Best Picture Oscar in 1934, the only time a comedy would do so until Woody Allen's *Annie Hall* in 1978. In fact, Capra received three Oscars for Best Director between 1932 and 1938, a rare honor for a director.

After he completed the successful Damon Runyon story *Lady for a Day* (1933), Capra's desire to leave fantasy and focus on social issues propelled him into a series of "message" films, such as *Mr. Deeds Goes to Town (1936), You Can't Take It With You* (1938), *Mr. Smith Goes to Washington* (1939), and *Meet John Doe* (1941). Each of these films deals with one man or one family pitted against established greed, corruption, and authority. In *Mr. Smith*, Capra hit gold with actor

Opposite: *It Happened One Night* (1934) starring Clark Gable and Claudette Colbert broke Oscar records and almost bankrupted the men's underwear industry. When Gable performed a striptease revealing nothing but a bare chest beneath his shirt, men stopped wearing undershirts. It wasn't until 1951 that Marlon Brando made them popular again in *A Streetcar Named Desire*.

Jimmy Stewart, who would help make *It's a Wonderful Life* (1946) perhaps the most memorable film of Capra's career.

It's Always Darkest Before the Dawn

Lighthearted depictions of the human condition have always needed a complement to survive. A new breed of directors learned to utilize film techniques in such a way as to frighten viewers through to their marrow by exposing the darker side of humanity and society.

Orson Welles's rich baritone became well recognized by radio audiences as the voice of Lamont Cranston in the mystery series *The Shadow*. His historic broadcast of H.G. Wells's *War of the Worlds* in October of 1938 fooled many radio listeners into thinking that martians had just invaded New Jersey, and generated throughout the New York area.

RKO brought Welles to Hollywood in 1940 when he was twenty-five and gave him full rein to do *Citizen Kane*. The film was a feat almost entirely of his own creation—Welles cowrote, produced, directed and acted in the project, as well as controlling editing, sound, and design. The controversy that surrounded the film's release echoed earlier shock waves associated with *The Birth of a Nation*. William Randolph

Opposite: Orson Welles, Hollywood's "enfant terrible" in action on the set of *Citizen Kane* (1941). Writer Dorothy Parker upon meeting the genius said: "It's like meeting God without dying."

Hearst instructed his newspapers not to take any ads from RKO after hearing that the film was about a Hearst-like publisher's climb to power. Welles threatened to sue both Hearst and RKO if *Kane* was suppressed by either one. That didn't stop Radio City Music Hall from refusing to show the film. The film lost $160,000 on its release and was not loved by audiences. A masterfully told story, it is widely regarded as one of finest and most influential films ever made.

Welles continued to produce his own works, often freelancing as an actor to raise necessary funds. His portrayal of the mysterious Rochester in the 1944 version of *Jane Eyre* still shines. His other productions include *The Stranger* (1946), *The Lady from Shanghai* (1948), *Macbeth* (1948), *Othello* (1952), *Mr. Arkadin* (1955), *Touch of Evil* (1958), *The Trial* (1963), and *Chimes at Midnight* (1966).

Another dark character, Alfred Hitchcock—the master of the macabre—came to the American forefront in the early 1940s after fifteen years of solid directing. His background was in the German studio style, but his experience was drawn from the British studio system.

Hitchcock's *The Man Who Knew Too Much* (1934), *The 39 Steps* (1935), and *The Lady Vanishes* (1938) brought him high notice. The macabre trademark that was to become synonymous with Hitchcock was the interspersing of sardonic humor with the gruesome or the mysterious. He used every cinematic trick in the book, such as tense musical scoring and the play of shadows. He became the master of suspense.

Hitchcock called upon the hidden talents of some of Hollywood's biggest names in his films, forever distorting the comfortable, established screen images of numerous favorite male stars. He turned the lighthearted, urbane sophisticate Cary Grant into a wife killer in *Suspicion* (1941) and a cat burglar in *To Catch a Thief* (1955). The affable, all-American war hero Jimmy Stewart became a voyeur in *Rear Window* (1954) and an obsessed neurotic in *Vertigo* (1958). Hitchcock also showcased such blonde Hollywood actresses such as Janet Leigh, Doris Day, Kim Novak, Eva Marie Saint, and Tippi Hedren. Grace Kelly, who appeared on the silver screen just eleven times, became a legendary leading lady for her roles in *Dial M for Murder* (1954), *Rear Window*, and *To Catch a Thief*.

As the 1950s wound to a close, there was a surge in movies with teenage themes catering to the burgeoning youth of the Baby Boom. Many of the films explored issues of premarital sex and rebellion, such as *Rebel Without A Cause* (1955), *Peyton Place* (1957), *A Summer Place* (1959) and *Blue Denim* (1959). The Production Code had already been tested by Otto Preminger in 1953 when he went ahead with *The Moon Is Blue*—a bedroom comedy whose dialogue crossed the line of so-called decency with such words as "virgin" and "pregnant."

Once Preminger proved that a film could succeed at the box office without the Code's approval, it was only a matter of time before other directors found ways to defy it. As the rigid morality inherent in the Code began to slip, a slew of transitional films emerged, grappling with such topics as drug addiction, rape, and incest. *The Man with the Golden Arm* (1955) is Preminger's examination of heroin addiction, *Anatomy of a Murder* (1959) an evocative and moody study of rape.

Also consumed with bringing out the darker side of life was Stanley Kubrick, a master director whose films portrayed both subtle and in-your-face horrors of society. His diverse works include *The Killing* (1956), *Paths of Glory*

Above: Thelma Ritter and Jimmy Stewart in Hitchcock's *Rear Window* (1954), one of the director's most provocative thrillers. Opposite: Alfred Hitchcock serves tea to leading lady Grace Kelly on the set of *To Catch a Thief* (1955). Hitchcock had a penchant for blonde actresses and Kelly was his hands-down favorite.

(1957), *Lolita* (1962), *Dr. Strangelove* (1964), *2001: A Space Odyssey* (1968), *A Clockwork Orange* (1971), *Barry Lyndon* (1975), *The Shining* (1980), and *Full Metal Jacket* (1987). Kubrick died shortly after the completion of his final film, *Eyes Wide Shut* (1999).

The dehumanization of man is one of Kubrick's recurring themes. His point of view is that social evils are human evils. Man created society, not the reverse. Without society, men kill individually, obeying their basic nature, but within society, men kill *en masse* in the name of flag waving and myriad "causes." These themes ring true in all of his films no matter how diverse.

Francis Ford Coppola first broke through in commercial filmmaking with the horror movie *Dementia 13* (1963). He learned cutting, dubbing, and writing from his mentor, producer-director Roger Corman. Coppola cowrote *Patton* (1970), for which he won the Academy Award for Best Screenplay—his first Oscar. His talent as an expansive filmmaker has been likened to that of Thomas Ince and D.W. Griffith. Coppola's passion for film is evident in his movies.

Perhaps his best-known and acclaimed work is his *Godfather* trilogy, based on the novels by Mario Puzo. *The Godfather* (1972) won the Academy Award for Best Picture. *The Godfather Part II* (1974) also won—an unprecedented feat for a sequel (this film is also the only sequel to appear on the American Film Institute's list of the top one hundred films of the first century of moviemaking). At the end of the 1970s, Coppola seized upon the controversial novel *Heart of*

Above: Marlon Brando as Don Corleone, playing in the garden with a grandchild shortly before his death in *The Godfather* (1972). In the 1960s Brando said: "The only reason I'm in Hollywood is because I don't have the moral courage to refuse the money."

Darkness, by Joseph Conrad, translating it into a more contemporary story and setting it in Vietnam for *Apocalypse Now* (1979).

The breadth of Coppola's talent as a director can be seen in the diversity of *The Cotton Club* (1984), *Peggy Sue Got Married* (1986), and *Bram Stoker's Dracula* (1992). Certainly,

he is a resilient filmmaker whose genius will continue to work its magic into the twenty-first century.

Like Coppola, Martin Scorsese often dances with the repulsive, and offers bleak situations in highly cinematic settings. His characters are, for the most part, inextricably enmeshed with their urban surroundings and social environments. *Mean Streets* (1973) provides a gruesome portrait of New York City's Little Italy. *Alice Doesn't Live Here Anymore* (1974) is a profile of the American Southwest, while *Taxi*

Above: Robert Duvall (left), Albert Hall (center), and Martin Sheen (right) in *Apocalypse Now* (1979), Francis Ford Coppola's updated version of Joseph Conrad's novel *Heart of Darkness*.

Driver (1976) returns to the frenzy and squalor of New York City at the time of the metropolis' decline in the 1970s.

Others films of Scorsese's examine, in a sometimes controversial fashion, the rise and fall of characters who are coping with their dubious situations in society, often generated by the darker side of their natures. *Raging Bull* (1980), The *Color of*

Money (1986), *The King of Comedy* (1983), *Goodfellas* (1990), *The Age of Innocence* (1993), *The Last Temptation of Christ* (1988), and *Casino* (1995) all masterfully depict these conflicts in various time periods.

Oliver Stone, a brash, passionately expressive director, began his career in the 1970s as a screenwriter. He won an Oscar for his screenplay for *Midnight Express* (1978), which gave him an in as a director for *The Hand* (1981)—an unfortunate bomb. He stayed in the business, cowriting *Conan the Barbarian* (1982) and writing *Scarface* (1983). He finally got another shot at directing with *Salvador* (1986), starring James Woods, which gained him some recognition. *Platoon* (1986), which had been delayed for years for a variety of reasons, earned four Oscars including Best Picture and Best Director. Surprisingly, it became a huge commercial success.

Stone's next film, *Wall Street* (1987), a splashy, study of capitalist corruption, became one of the most powerful indictments of 1980s avarice and junk-bond dealers. Stone earned further accolades and yet another Best Director Oscar for *Born on the Fourth of July* (1989). Seemingly at home with excessive controversy, Stone continues to draw personal attention through such recent films as *JFK, The Doors* (both 1991), *Natural Born Killers* (1994), and *Nixon* (1995).

Opposite: Diane Keaton (left) flirts with Woody Allen (right) in *Annie Hall* (1977), considered by many to be Allen's finest and most innovative film. The oft quoted Allen has said "I don't want to achieve immortality through my art. I want to achieve immortality through not dying."

Classics of Comedy

Hollywood has always been as full of humor as it is full of moodiness, darkness, and fear. Perhaps one of the most laugh-provoking directors of the twentieth century is Woody Allen. Like Chaplin's Little Tramp, the Woody Allen persona crops up in countless movies under various names, but always as the same nerdy schlemiel who, although desperate to fit into social contrivances, remains an outsider looking in. The Allen persona longs for universal acceptance, but he is also critical of most social institutions—hence his personal neuroses. While Allen detractors deplore his seeming self-obsession, fans recognize the axiom, "write what you know."

Allen emerged in the 1950s as a television comedy writer and a stand-up comedian, but following the success of *What's New, Pussycat?* (1965)—which he wrote and acted in—he plunged into filmmaking and screenwriting, scoring hit after hit with such films as *Take the Money and Run* (1969), *Bananas* (1971), *Everything You Always Wanted to Know About Sex (But Were Afraid to Ask)* (1972), and *Sleeper* (1973). *Annie Hall* (1977) was a breakthrough film for Allen and won him an Academy Award for Best Picture—the first film comedy to do so since Capra's *It Happened One Night*. The film also ran away with Best Director, Best Screenplay, and Best Actress (Diane Keaton) honors.

After *Annie Hall*, Allen worked at a frantic pace. *Manhattan* (1979) was another relationship story set in New York City.

Allen revisited everything from old vaudevillians in *Broadway Danny Rose* (1984) to the Depression in *The Purple Rose of Cairo* (1985) to the golden age of radio in *Radio Days* (1987). He continued to play with various classic film genres, such as film noir in *Shadows and Fog* (1992), and the Hollywood musical in *Everyone Says I Love You* (1996). In 1998, he entered the realm of animation, performing the voice for the lead character in *Antz*. Also in 1998, Allen tackled the world of Hollywood debauchery with his film *Celebrity*.

Mel Brooks was a onetime stand-up comic who was hired by Sid Caesar to write for his weekly television program, *Your Show of Shows*. He made his directorial debut with *The Producers* (1967) and earned an Academy Award for Best Screenplay. He soon signed up with Warner Bros. to make the classics *Blazing Saddles* (1974), written with Richard Pryor and others *Young Frankenstein* (1974), a spoof penned with Gene Wilder, who also had a starring role; and *Silent Movie* (1976), written with Barry Levinson. His other memorable films include *High Anxiety* (1977), *History of the World—Part I* (1981), and *Spaceballs* (1987), the latter being a send-up of the *Star Wars* trilogy.

Actor-writer-producer-director Carl Reiner also wrote for *Your Show of Shows*, and he created *The Dick Van Dyke Show*, for which he won five Emmys. He entered the world of film in the early 1960s, writing *The Thrill of It All* (1963) and *The Art of Love* (1965)—both directed by Norman Jewison. After a time-out of almost ten years, Reiner waded into films again, this time boosting comic Steve Martin's career with such

comedies as *The Jerk* (1979), *The Man With Two Brains* (1983), and *All of Me* (1984). In addition to featured roles in numerous films, Reiner has made countless cameo appearances.

Rob Reiner, Carl's son, first became known for his role as Mike "Meathead" Styvick in *All in the Family*, but since then, the actor-turned-director has shown his repertoire encompasses more than comedy. In addition to directing *This Is Spinal Tap* (1984), *The Princess Bride* (1987), and *When Harry Met Sally* (1989), he also steered the ship for *A Few Good Men* (1992).

Holy Blockbuster, Batman!

A group of relatively young directors sparked the blockbuster trend in the mid to late 1970s—and this trend has remained strong, thanks to ticket-buyers' yearning for fantasy and edge-of-your-seat thrills.

The young pioneer of the blockbuster genre, baby boomer Steven Spielberg was dubbed the "wunderkind" of the movie world when he came to international prominence with the groundbreaking *Jaws* (1975) at the mere age of twenty-seven. He followed that success with the sci-fi film *Close Encounters of the Third Kind* (1977), another massive victory.

As Spielberg entered the 1980s, he moved to directing adventure films such as *Raiders of the Lost Ark* (1981) and its sequels, *Indiana Jones and the Temple of Doom* (1984) and *Indiana Jones and the Last Crusade* (1989). The fantasy

E.T. The Extra-Terrestrial (1982) was the highest grossing film of all time until James Cameron's *Titanic* surpassed it in 1998.

Steering away from the kinds of films that made him famous, Spielberg directed *The Color Purple* (1985), based on the novel by Alice Walker, and received great reviews, showing he could do more than just dazzle an audience with special effects and fantasy. *Hook* (1991) was billed as the next Spielberg blockbuster, but it fared badly at the box office. However, the legendary director quickly redeemed himself with *Jurassic Park* (1993), a box-office smash.

Spielberg decided to tackle a deeply serious and disturbing subject—the Holocaust—with *Schindler's List* (1993). The film

was lauded as a masterpiece and won seven Academy Awards. Upon receiving his statuette for Best Director, Spielberg gave a moving account of what led him to attempt such a film. As he later reflected, it would be a difficult challenge to see where he could go from there.

Amistad (1997), which deals with a dark chapter in American history—slavery—opened to critical acclaim and was recognized by the Academy. But its power was quickly overshadowed by the blockbuster *Titanic* (1998). Undaunted, Spielberg addressed yet another harrowing aspect of World

Below: Kate Winslet (left) and Leonardo DiCaprio (center) take direction from James Cameron (right) on the set of *Titanic* (1997). The film broke records for budget, box-office receipts, and Academy Awards.

War II—the D-Day invasion—and recreated the bloody landing on Omaha Beach in Normandy for *Saving Private Ryan* (1998). The film caused a tremendous stir as it depicted realistic and explicit gore and recounted horrendous casualties by means of hand-held camera technique and nauseating special effects. For this particular achievement, Spielberg earned a second Academy Award for Best Director. He will continue to tackle issues in films that teach history to future generations while entertaining audiences at the same time.

Also a member of the boy-wonder blockbuster set, George Lucas wrote a script with college friends that recalled the good old days of drive-ins and hot rods. Francis Ford Coppola, who had produced Lucas's first experimental sci-fi film, *THX 1138*, in 1971, agreed to produce *American Graffiti* (1973), a low-budget film that yielded extraordinary returns.

Lucas's most memorable—and profitable—project, *Star Wars* (1977), was a monumental risk that a number of studios were afraid to touch, but because the epic contained broad family appeal and was like nothing audiences had seen before, it ended up setting a new all-time box-office record, earning $193 million dollars—50 percent more than *Jaws*. *Star Wars* made use of brand-new effects techniques that spawned other science-fiction films. It was followed by *The Empire Strikes Back* (1980) and *Return of the Jedi* (1983). All three films were re-released in early 1997—complete with enhanced sound, new scenes, and additional effects—for a new generation of audiences to enjoy on the big screen. The

newest film in the saga, *Star Wars: Episode I—The Phantom Menace*, released in May 1999, featured an all-star cast, including Liam Neeson, Samuel L. Jackson, Natalie Portman, and Ewan McGregor.

In 1989, thirty-one-year-old Tim Burton brought comic books to life—and created lines around the corner at movie theaters—with *Batman*. The movie sparked numerous sequels (though only the first, *Batman Returns,* was directed by Burton), with every big name in Hollywood vying for the roles of the classic villains; Jack Nicholson played The Joker in the original film, while such stars as Tommy Lee Jones (Two-Face), Jim Carrey (The Riddler), Arnold Schwarzenegger (Mr. Freeze), and Uma Thurman (Poison Ivy) starred in later films.

Burton's exceptional talent was first noticed by Disney, which hired him to direct two short films—*Vincent* (1982), which he completed at the tender age of twenty-four, and, *Frankenweenie* (1984). *Pee-wee's Big Adventure* established the young director in 1985. Burton's trademark style hinges on the highly original and surreal as evidenced by *Beetle Juice* (1988), *Edward Scissorhands* (1990) and *Ed Wood* (1994).

James Cameron, writer and director of *The Terminator* (1984), *Terminator 2: Judgment Day* (1991), and *True Lies* (1994), now sits on top of the heap with the spectacular success of his latest film, *Titanic* (1997). Cameron is well known for his incredible expenditures, but *Titanic* set a record with a budget of $230 million. *Titanic* also shook up the Academy, reeling in a record number of Oscars in 1998.

Above: Denzel Washington (right) delivers an Academy Award–worthy performance as the radical activist in Spike Lee's *Malcolm X.*

Rogue Directors

In the spirit of the first directorial pioneers, a new breed of filmmakers emerged in the 1980s and 1990s, pushing the envelope with every new picture.

When Spike Lee burst out with *She's Gotta Have It* in 1986, his talents as a producer, writer, director, and actor were easily recognizable. *School Daze* (1988), partly financed by Columbia, allowed Lee to stir up controversy by examining black cultural divisions and stereotypes, causing some resentment in the black community.

Do the Right Thing (1989) established Lee as an original filmmaker and earned him an Oscar nomination for Best Screenplay. His next project, *Mo' Better Blues* (1990), was a look at the life of a jazz musician. His stereotypical depiction of Jewish nightclub owners brought criticism. With *Jungle Fever* (1991), Lee sparked even more debate over his examination of an interracial love affair.

Lee's *Malcolm X* (1992), starring Denzel Washington, offers a more objective historical look at one of the country's most powerful and flamboyant black activists. Lee made use of semi-documentary techniques to give the film an added measure of realism. While some critics felt that Lee was too

Above: Dennis Hopper inhales some ether while simultaneously battering his favorite victim, Isabella Rossellini, in David Lynch's dark and sadistic *Blue Velvet* (1986). Says Hopper: "People keep asking me, 'what evil lurks in you to play such bad characters?' There is no evil. I just wear tight underwear."

gentle with Malcolm X's shady beginnings as a hustler, Lee's attempts to depict the contemporary significance of the leader's life and times made for a satisfying film. Lee's next films, *Crooklyn* (1994) and *Clockers* (1995), were also well received.

The Coen Brothers are rogue filmmakers of another kind. By exploring the boundaries of every film genre imaginable, the Coens have carved a unique niche for their work. As a result, they are among the most acclaimed contemporary filmmakers. Joel Coen, born in 1954, writes and directs. Ethan Coen, born in 1957, writes and produces. Together, they have accomplished in fifteen years what few achieve in a lifetime, consistently surprising audiences with films so varied that the only way to know they're by the same team is to check the credits.

The brothers caught immediate attention with their 1984 debut, *Blood Simple.* In *Raising Arizona* (1987), starring Nicolas Cage and Holly Hunter, the pair pay homage to screwball comedy. *Miller's Crossing* (1990), inspired by Dashiell Hammett, is an engrossing, lavish gangster drama starring Gabriel Byrne and Albert Finney. In *Barton Fink* (1991), the Coens come dangerously close to engaging the audience with tragic characters—but they deliberately stop short. *Fargo* (1996) earned critical acclaim and box-office success, as well as a nod from the Acadamy. *The Big Lebowski* followed in 1998.

Quentin Tarantino's work virtually leapt off the screen in the early 1990s. Prior to writing and directing, he was a video store clerk with an actor's background. Perhaps it's just as well that his disturbed fantasies have found a creative outlet, although one should be warned before attempting to view his first film, *Reservoir Dogs* (1992).

Tarantino next wrote two screenplays: *True Romance* (1993), directed by Tony Scott, and *Natural Born Killers* (1994), directed by Oliver Stone. (Tarantino's script for the latter was revised, and he did not receive a credit.)

Tarantino's masterpiece to date is undoubtedly the raunchy, comically—and excessively—violent *Pulp Fiction* (1994). Written and directed by Tarantino, the film has a complex narrative structure that was more than enough to earn it the Palme D'Or at the Cannes Film Festival.

Tales of the bizarre, the unexpected, and oftentimes the grotesque are associated with cult filmmaker David Lynch. Considered one of the most daring and experimental of the underground, Lynch successfully moved between cult and mainstream status.

Lynch made his debut in 1978 with *Eraserhead*, a motion picture filled with abhorrent images of bodily functions and sex. He took his sense of the grotesque to the mainstream with *The Elephant Man* (1980), which starred John Hurt as John (Joseph) Merrick, the true-life deformed young Englishman who lived in London at the end of the nineteenth century. *In Blue Velvet* (1986), Lynch found the vehicle that would best showcase his talents. The film is a brooding, erotic, and voyeuristic look into the sexually gruesome and terrifying.

HOLLYWOOD'S BRIGHTEST STARS

Stars are not born—they're made. The first movie moguls may have initiated the movie star trend, but over the years, stars have ultimately made themselves. When the star system kicked in, actors and actresses became the people we wanted them to be, both onscreen and off. An unknown plucked from obscurity was fastidiously groomed for the job of star, completely made over to suit the studio's requirements. Family histories were hidden when necessary—even obliterated. New personal histories were created. As is still true today, names were changed to have appeal.

Early audiences read the hype in motion picture fan magazines, such as *Photoplay*, as early as 1912, making it clear that they believed—or wanted to believe—the screen images. It was becoming next to impossible to separate the real actors from their fictionalized identities. The studios pushed their stars into acting out the fictions. In a bid to give the people what they wanted, studio publicists spread grandiose stories about the stars' lavish lifestyles, and soon screen goddesses showed up at premieres in fancy limousines accompanied by Russian wolfhounds, whose fur was dyed to match their gowns. And the stars themselves began to buy into the publicity machines. Many of them were consumed by their own auras, living in a world completely disassociated from reality. It was next to impossible for them to ignore the adulation of the public. Marlene Dietrich, as large a legend in her own mind as in anyone else's, once said, "Look at how many ugly people there are in this world. No wonder they pay us so much money."

In this section, we'll profile the actors and actresses who stole the hearts of American moviegoers and became movie legends.

The First Movie
STARS

When Carl Laemmle rescued Florence Lawrence from obscurity as the Biograph Girl and made her a star in her own right, he encouraged other star players to reach for greater fame and fortune. Actors were soon to realize annual salaries of a million dollars—unheard-of wealth in those days. Other stars followed suit.

"Little" Mary Pickford became known as America's Sweetheart. The persona of dashing swashbuckler fit Douglas Fairbanks's square-jawed good looks, whereas Rudolph Valentino best expressed the sensitive, sensual Latin lover. The virginal woman became synonymous with Lillian Gish, while a more sophisticated tragedienne was to be found in Gloria Swanson. The "fat man" was Fattie Arbuckle, while the role of the people's champion was embodied by Charlie Chaplin, Buster Keaton, and Harold Lloyd.

Starlets

The test case of Theda Bara revolutionized Hollywood's star system. And it was all due to William Fox, who had bought a play called *A Fool There Was* based on Rudyard Kipling's poem "The Vampire." To play the lead, director Frank Powell selected Theodosia Goodman, a rather plump Jewish girl from Cincinnati who preferred "legitimate" stage work. Economic circumstances pushed her to Hollywood, where she was cast in Fox's film as a hotly sensual femme fatale, who devours men then tosses them aside. Fox knew that a nice Jewish girl from Cincinnati was not the image to give to the public. So, with the aid of his publicist, he created an exotic persona—Theda Bara, the famous French actress whose father, a French artist, had moved to Egypt, where he met her mother. Young Theda, so the story went, grew up at the foot of the Sphinx and spent her early years flying across the desert on a camel, her dark hair streaming, with a group of Arab nomads. The hype was released before the film and audiences ate it up. When *A Fool There Was* (1915) premiered and audiences read the famous line, "Kiss me, my fool," Theda Bara became an overnight success.

Thereafter, she was referred to as "the Vamp," and that word officially entered the English language. Photo stills of "the Vamp" grew more seductive each year as Theda Bara's mystique gathered steam. Poses with skulls, snakes, and Egyptian figurines sucked the public in. Bara's films, regardless of content, played up her "vamp" persona.

Pages 50-51: Katharine Hepburn and David Manners in *A Bill of Divorcement* (1932), her film debut.

Page 52: Silent-screen star Rudolf Valentino's smoldering sexuality made female audiences melt. When he died suddenly at age thirty-one, mass hysteria ensued.

Page 53: Harold Lloyd in the classic comedy *Safety Last* (1923). Lloyd was remarkably agile and performed most of his stunts without help.

Opposite: Lillian Gish was one of D.W. Griffith's favorite actresses, portraying the waifish and innocent heroine in most of her early silent films. On her longstanding appeal, Gish remarked, "I've never been in style so I can't go out of style."

American woman. She achieved both stardom and success in such silent films as *Rough House Rosie* (1927), *Red Hair* (1928), *Three Weekends* (1928), *The Saturday Night Kid* (1929), *Call Her Savage* (1932), and *Hoopla* (1933).

She arrived in Hollywood from Brooklyn, New York, while still in her teens. Her first films included *Beyond the Rainbow* (1922), *Daughters of Pleasure* (1924), and *The Adventurous Sex* (1925). Bow was dubbed the "It Girl," as she was chosen by British author Elinor Glyn to appear in the movie based on her book about "It"—not sex and sexual attraction as most Americans mistook it, but personal magnetism, charm, and charisma.

Unfortunately Bow froze in front of microphones, and her heavy Brooklyn accent was a liability to her "It-ness" when the new "talkies" invaded the silent screen. She left pictures in 1933 in a veil of personal scandals, which contributed to her fall from popularity.

Although she was known as America's Sweetheart, Mary Pickford was so much more. In addition to being a remarkable dramatic actress, she was a sharp businesswoman who produced many of her own pictures, negotiated contracts for herself and other stars, and was one of the founders of United Artists (with soon-to-be-husband Douglas Fairbanks, D.W. Griffith, and Charlie Chaplin) in 1919.

Born Gladys Smith in Toronto, Canada, Pickford began her career on the stage when she was five as "Baby Gladys Smith." She changed her name in 1907 and signed on with Biograph in 1909. She moved from company to company as "the girl

After four years of constant vamping, Bara wanted different roles, but the public and the studio had locked her into a stereotype. Bitter, despite a weekly salary in excess of four thousand dollars, Goodman bowed out. She married and lived quietly thereafter.

Clara Bow was the first genuine flapper of the Roaring Twenties, embodying the vivacious and newly emancipated

Above: Clara Bow, dubbed the "It Girl" by author Elinor Glyn, personified the newly emancipated woman of the 1920s flapper era.

with the golden curls" and was a box-office success. Her films include the silents *Rebecca of Sunnybrook Farm* (1917), *Stella Maris* (1918), *Little Lord Fauntleroy* (1921), in which she played both mother and son, and *My Best Girl* (1927), which costarred her future husband, Charles "Buddy" Rogers.

Pickford didn't fare as well in "talkies" and retired from screen acting in 1933, but became active in radio throughout the 1930s. In 1953, she sold her interest in United Artists.

Possibly the original "waif" actress, Lillian Gish began her career at the age of five. In 1912, Mary Pickford introduced her to D.W. Griffith, who cast them as on-screen siblings in *An Unseen Enemy*. She became the embodiment of the Griffith heroine, starring in *The Birth of a Nation* (1915) and *Intolerance* (1916). She reached her career summit in such films as *Hearts of the World* (1918), *True Heart Susie* (1919), *Broken Blossoms* (1919), *Way Down East* (1920), and *Orphans of the Storm* (1922). After making her first talkie, *One Romantic Night* (1930), Gish returned to the stage.

She came back to Hollywood in 1942, playing character roles until one of her last parts, a cameo in Robert Altman's *A Wedding*, in 1978. She also appeared in several TV movies in the 1980s. Gish's final screen role was opposite Bette Davis in 1987's *Whales of August*.

Born in Chicago, Illinois, Gloria Swanson (née Swenson) came to Hollywood in 1915. Perhaps best remembered for her role as Nora Desmond in *Sunset Blvd.* (1950), Swanson actually began her film career as a comedienne. She played slapstick in *The Danger Girl* (1916) and *Teddy at the Throttle*

(1917), but yearned for dramatic roles. When she was discovered by Cecil B. DeMille, her dreams became a reality. He cast her in *Don't Change Your Husband* and *Male and Female*, both released in 1919, and made her a star. She received her first Oscar nomination for her role in *Sadie Thompson* (1928).

The introduction of sound into motion pictures worked for Swanson. She received an Oscar nomination for her first talkie, *The Trespasser* (1928). But after a couple of successful musicals in the early 1930s, her career began to decline. Although she made several films in the 1930s and 1940s, these did nothing to boost her popularity at the box office. Despite her memorable performance as Norma Desmond in *Sunset Blvd.* which won her an Oscar nomination, her film career was pretty much over.

Silent Heros

The phenomenon of Rudolph Valentino can only be likened to a dam of sexual awakening that burst open, rendering existing sensibilities asunder. Audiences beheld the young Valentino, whose dark, smoldering eyes and lithe physique offered raw passion, sexuality, and tragedy. They also sensed that having been drawn inexorably into this nameless passion, there could be no retreat.

Valentino was born in Castellaneta, Italy, in 1895. He came to the United States in 1913, making his living as a landscape gardener, a gigolo, and a petty criminal before becoming a ballroom dancer. He arrived in Hollywood in 1917, appearing in such films as *Society Sensation* (1918), *Eyes of Youth* (1919), *Once to Every Woman* (1920), and *The Four Horsemen of the Apocalypse* (1921), which became a hit.

In *The Sheik* (1921), he demonstrated his dancer's grace with easy, fluid movement. *Blood and Sand* (1922) placed him in the middle of an aura of tragic and vulnerable sexual appetites. He starred in *The Eagle* (1925) and then *The Son of the Sheik* (1926), conquering female hearts around the globe. His was an honest sensuality. He held nothing back. The media wondered if he was slightly effeminate, especially when compared to Douglas Fairbanks.

Before Valentino could alleviate any doubts about his masculinity, he died suddenly at the age of thirty-one from a ruptured ulcer. Worldwide hysteria ensued, along with several suicides. There was rioting at his funeral, where people lined some eleven blocks to view the body.

Douglas Fairbanks almost never made it to Hollywood. Although he started a career on the stage in the early part of the twentieth century, he gave it all up to get married and raise a family, joining a Wall Street brokerage firm in 1907. But he couldn't stay away from the stage, and he began acting on Broadway again after his son was born in 1909. Hollywood beckoned, and by 1919, he had formed United Artists with his soon-to-be second wife, Mary Pickford, as well as D.W. Griffith and Charlie Chaplin.

Fairbanks made a name for himself as the screen's first swashbuckling hero and became famous for his roles in such films as *The Mark of Zorro* (1920), *The Three Musketeers* (1921), *Robin Hood* (1922), and *The Thief of Bagdad* (1924). *The Black Pirate* (1926) presented some of Fairbanks's greatest stunts. His last film was *The Private Life of Don Juan* in 1934.

Comic Geniuses

Charlie Chaplin knew all about poverty, class systems, and loss (his father had died while he was a boy, and his mother spent most of her life in mental institutions). As a child, he literally sang for his supper, as he and his older half brother Sydney took acting jobs to support his mother. At the age of seventeen, Chaplin joined a theater company that brought him to the United States. In 1912, he met up with Mack Sennett, who hired him almost immediately. Chaplin made his directorial debut on his thirteenth film, *Caught in the Rain* (1914). By 1919, he had formed United Artists with Mary Pickford, Douglas Fairbanks, and D.W. Griffith.

Chaplin's most famous creation is his character the Little Tramp, who evokes tenderness, poignancy, and whimsy. Chaplin described him as "a gentleman, a poet, a dreamer, a lonely fellow always hopeful of romance and adventure." Hoping for redemption or transformation through love, the

Opposite: Douglas Fairbanks, shown here in *The Black Pirate* (1926), was Hollywood's first action hero, starring in swashbuckling adventures that showcased his athletic prowess as a stuntman. A rugged leading man, he typified the "all-American" suitor in contrast to Valentino's lithe Latin sensuality.

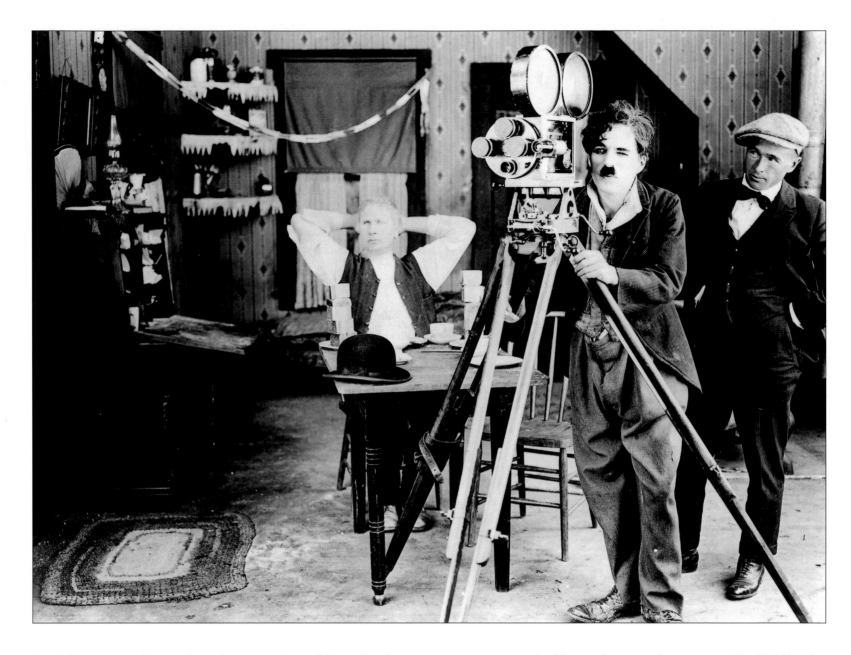

Little Tramp usually winds up losing in the end. Faced with his loss, he is forced to look at it philosophically and assume his more carefree self once again. This type of narrative is what made Chaplin's Little Tramp so universally appealing and remarkably poignant.

Using the barest of set decoration and without any trick photography, Chaplin concentrated the camera's focus on his own comical gestures. A perfectionist, he is said to have spent two weeks filming the pancake scene in *The Kid* (1921), in which he uses his blanket as a robe. He shot fifty thousand feet (15,240m) of film and used only seventy-five (23m).

Above: Charlie Chaplin's Little Tramp's universal appeal is marked by a pathos revealed through a love story. The Tramp, hoping for redemption or transformation through love, usually winds up losing in the end. Faced with his loss, he is forced to look at it philosophically and ultimately, he assumes his carefree self once more.

Chaplin was horrified with the advent of talking films. He stated, "Motion pictures need dialogue as much as Beethoven symphonies need lyrics." He ignored sound and continued making successful silent films in the 1930s, such as *City Lights* (1931) and *Modern Times* (1936), adding only musical sound tracks. His first sound comedy emerged in 1940 with *The Great Dictator*. Chaplin made few movies following the sound revolution, and after he was refused a reentry visa to the United States in 1952, he vowed never to return. He did make one final appearance, however, in 1972, when he was awarded a Lifetime Achievement Oscar.

Known to many as "the king of daredevil comedy," Harold Lloyd was remarkably agile and performed most of his stunts without any help whatsoever. Lloyd began his movie career as an extra for the Edison Company in 1912. In 1915, he hooked up with friend Hal Roach and made the shorts *Just Nuts* (1915) and *Stop! Look! Listen!* (1917). Unfortunately for Lloyd, he and his characters were usually viewed as second-string compared to Chaplin, but he continued to make many films in the 1920s, such as the classic *Safety Last* (1923). When sound came on the scene, he readily adapted with such films as *Welcome Danger* (1929), *Feet First* (1931), and *Movie Crazy* (1932), but as a new era of comedy started to arise in the 1930s, Lloyd lost his place on the comic screen. His last film role was the lead in *The Sin of Harold Diddlebock* in 1947, though he lived twenty-four more years.

Whereas Harold Lloyd set himself up as the butt of the humor in his films, Buster Keaton did quite the opposite, preferring to focus upon the hilarity of society. Keaton's view was that it was society who forced a decent fellow into ridiculous postures and behaviors.

Keaton entered the world of film in 1917, after he met Roscoe "Fatty" Arbuckle in a New York City studio and made his debut in *The Butcher Boy* (1917), which starred Arbuckle. When Arbuckle moved to Hollywood, Keaton followed. Keaton liked to pit his acrobatic talents against objects for comical effect. He was a superb stuntman and worked outdoors using real props, such as locomotives or bridges, rather than miniatures drawn to scale.

A one-time carnival performer from Kansas, Roscoe "Fatty" Arbuckle got into movies in 1908. His appearance made him seem a natural for slapstick comedy, and he signed with Mack Sennett in 1913. In 1917, Arbuckle launched his own production company. The films he made—with hired comic talent Buster Keaton—included *Out West* (1918), *Back Stage* (1919), *The Roundup* (1920), and *Brewster's Millions* (1921).

Scandal got the best of Arbuckle in 1921, when newspapers reported on a party that Arbuckle had supposedly thrown in 1917—immediately after which Arbuckle had paid a district attorney $100,000, ostensibly as a gift. Apparently, one of the guests was found dead in her bedroom, victim of a vicious rape. A week later Arbuckle surrendered to the police and was tried for involuntary manslaughter. Ultimately, Arbuckle was found not guilty but this verdict did not spare him in the eyes of the public. His career was over.

Leading
LADIES

Drama Queens

By age sixteen, Joan Crawford was working on Broadway and in an after-hours nightclub, where she was discovered by an MGM executive. She made her first film, *Pretty Ladies*, in 1925, but it was *Our Dancing Daughters* (1928) that launched her into stardom.

Over the next few years, Crawford gave memorable performances in *Mildred Pierce* (1945), which won her an Oscar, *Humoresque* (1946), and *Possessed* (1947), for which she received an Oscar nomination. In the 1950s, she starred in *Sudden Fear* (1952), and *Torch Song* (1953), among others. In 1955, she married Pepsi-Cola chairman Alfred Steele, and after his death, she remained on the company's board. In 1962, she made a comeback performance opposite Bette Davis in *What*

Page 62: Lauren Bacall rocketed to stardom at nineteen after director Howard Hawks cast her opposite Humphrey Bogart in *To Have and Have Not* (1944). Hawks told Bogie: "We are going to try an interesting thing. You are about the most insolent man on the screen, and I'm going to make this girl a little more insolent than you are."

Page 63: Audrey Hepburn's unique poise and refinement coupled with her endearing charm and trend-setting fashions, earned her a special place in audiences' hearts.

Right: Joan Crawford embodied the strong-willed, glamorous, and ambitious woman of the 1940s. She took her job seriously: "I never go out unless I look like Joan Crawford the movie star. If you want to see the girl next door, go next door."

Hollywood's
Brightest
Stars

Ever Happened to Baby Jane, which launched her into a series of horror films, including *Strait-Jacket* (1964), *I Saw What You Did* (1965), *Berserk* (1967), and *Trog* (1970), her last film.

Although Crawford was adored throughout her career, her daughter, Christina, published a book, *Mommie Dearest*, a year after her death in 1977, marring the legendary actress' public image. The book, which was made into a film of the same name, depicted Crawford as an abusive mother.

Bette Davis's film career, which began in the 1930s and spanned forty years, was studded with Oscar-winning portrayals of intensely sensitive and neurotic women. After making several uneventful films in the early 1930s, Davis landed a role in *Of Human Bondage* (1934), which got her career rolling. Her role in *Dangerous* in 1935 earned her an Academy Award. The next few years provided her with some of her most memorable films, including *Jezebel* (1938), for which she won another Oscar, *Dark Victory* (1939), *The Letter* (1940), and *The Little Foxes* (1941).

In the 1950s, Davis added two more memorable characters to her lengthy résumé. In *All About Eve* (1950), she played a powerful Broadway star whose status is undermined by a conniving wannabe. And in *The Virgin Queen* (1955), Davis once again assumed the aura of England's Elizabeth I as she had done so successfully in 1939 with *The Private Lives of Elizabeth and Essex*. Davis worked beyond the 1950s, mostly in character roles, but even these slowly disappeared. With Hollywood structures and tastes crumbling, things looked grim. She felt compelled to advertise for a job in *Variety* in 1962, and spent

her final years of her career making TV movies. Her last motion picture, made with Lillian Gish, was *Whales of August* (1987).

The incredibly talented Vivien Leigh's immortalized one of literature's most spirited heroines, Scarlett O'Hara, in *Gone With the Wind (1939)*. She had made her debut in *Things Are Looking Up* in 1934 and met the love of her life when she starred opposite Laurence Olivier in *Fire Over England* (1937). David Selznick was a his wit's end in his search for the perfect Scarlett when Oliver introduced him to Leigh in 1938. He quickly cast her in the coveted role, for which she won her first of two Oscars.

Leigh made several more films in the 1940s—*Waterloo Bridge* (1940), *That Hamilton Woman* (1941), and *Caesar and Cleopatra* (1946) among them. In 1948, she portrayed the doomed Tolstoy heroine in *Anna Karenina*. She won her second Oscar for her role as Blanche Dubois in the film adaption of Tennessee Williams's *A Streetcar Named Desire* (1951). Her long battle with tuberculosis limited the number of films she was able to do, but she managed to give memorable performances in *The Deep Blue Sea* (1955), *The Roman Spring of Mrs. Stone* (1961), and *Ship of Fools* (1965).

More than Scarlett's faithful friend Melanie in *Gone With the Wind*, Olivia de Havilland began her film career with *A Midsummer Night's Dream* in 1935. For her next film, *Captain*

Opposite: Carl Laemmle once described Bette Davis as having "about as much sex appeal as Slim Summerville." But Davis, shown here with Gary Merrill in *All About Eve* (1950), used her unique presence to her advantage, and became one of the most respected actresses in Hollywood.

Blood (1935), she was paired with Errol Flynn, with whom she would make a total of ten films at Warner Bros. After her Academy Award–nominated performance in *Gone With the Wind*, de Havilland returned to Warner, making several more films in the 1940s, including *Hold Back the Dawn* (1941). She was nominated for another Academy Award, but lost to her sister Joan Fontaine, who won it for *Suspicion* (1941).

In the 1950s, de Havilland left Hollywood for Broadway, but returned to films from time to time, performing in *Lady in a Cage* (1964), *Hush…Hush, Sweet Charlotte* (1964), and *Pope Joan* (1972), among others. She made a couple of TV movies, including *The Royal Romance* (1982), in which she played England's Queen Mother, Elizabeth.

Timeless Beauties

Although her Hollywood career spanned only six years and eleven films, Grace Kelly is one of Hollywood's most beloved leading ladies. A shy and awkward product of a middle-class Philadelphia family, Kelly went on to epitomize Hollywood style, glamour, and yes, grace.

Like many film stars before her—and after—Kelly's dream was to be a stage actress. But she found herself in Hollywood with the assistance of her playwright uncle, George Kelly. Her first role, in the movie *Fourteen Hours* (1951), was small, but

Opposite: The regal Grace Kelly played the Katharine Hepburn role (Tracy Lord) in *High Society* (1956), the musical adaption of *The Philadelphia Story*.

it led her to be cast opposite Gary Cooper in the classic 1952 western *High Noon*. This role launched her to a stardom that allowed her to choose her own roles and play opposite the likes of Clark Gable, in *Mogambo* (1953), and Bing Crosby, in *The Country Girl* (1954), winning an Oscar for the latter. She will perhaps be best remembered as Alfred Hitchcock's darling, starring in such films as *Dial M for Murder* (1954), *Rear Window* (1954), and *To Catch a Thief* (1955).

Kelly's last Hollywood appearances were in 1956, opposite Frank Sinatra in *High Society* and in the prophetic role of a woman engaged to a prince in *The Swan*. In 1957, she married Prince Rainer of Monaco and left "Grace Kelly" behind to become Princess Grace. She died in a car accident in 1982.

Elizabeth Taylor was a child star who came to prominence with *Lassie Come Home* (1943). Costar Roddy McDowall often recounted a favorite story about meeting this girl with startling violet eyes. Apparently, after interviewing young Elizabeth, a studio executive told her to go home and wash off the heavy mascara. Taylor had to explain that her lashes were completely her own.

Taylor made a long succession of films, almost all them successful. She inched her way into adulthood through such vehicles as *Jane Eyre* (1944), *National Velvet* (1944), and *Little Women* (1949). In 1950, she played the starry-eyed daughter of Spencer Tracy in *Father of the Bride*. Several films followed in quick succession, including *A Place in the Sun* (1951), *Ivanhoe* (1952), *The Last Time I Saw Paris* (1954), *Giant* (1956), *Cat on a Hot Tin Roof* (1958), *Suddenly, Last Summer*

(1959), and *Butterfield 8* (1960), for which she won her first Academy Award. As her career soared, she changed from a breathtaking debutante to a full-blown siren. She broke new ground in terms of salary, publicity, and length of production with *Cleopatra* in 1963. She starred in several films with two-time husband Richard Burton, including 1966's *Who's Afraid Of Virginia Woolf*, for which she won a second Oscrar.

Born Edda Hepburn-Ruston in Brussels, Audrey Hepburn began her American acting career on Broadway in the title role of *Gigi* in 1952. Signed by director William Wyler to film on location in Rome, she made her Hollywood debut with *Roman Holiday* in 1953. In an almost unheard of feat for a first film, Hepburn won an Oscar for her memorable performance as Princess Anne. After that, her career was set in motion, but she was very discriminating about the roles she accepted.

In 1954, Hepburn starred opposite Humphrey Bogart in *Sabrina*. She played Natasha in *War and Peace* (1956) and danced and sang with Fred Astaire in *Funny Face* in 1957. That same year, she also starred in *Love in the Afternoon*. Her roles for the next few years found her soaring on top of Hollywood's A-list: *The Nun's Story* (1959), for which she received an Oscar nomination; *The Unforgiven* (1960); and *Breakfast at Tiffany's* (1961), another Academy-recognized performance. *Charade* (1963) and *My Fair Lady* (1964) kept her in the limelight. The thriller *Wait Until Dark* (1967) would be her last Hollywood film for a decade.

In the late 1960s Hepburn left acting to devote time to her family. In 1976 she returned to the screen opposite Sean Connery in *Robin and Marian*. In the early 1980s she turned her attention to UNICEF and became its international goodwill ambassador. Hollywood had not forgotten its darling, however: a few months after her death in 1993, the Academy awarded her the Jean Hersholt Humanitarian Award.

Coyly Controversial

Dubbed "box-office poison" for several of her roles, and probably the most controversial actress in Hollywood, Katharine Hepburn has created a legacy for strong women who speak their minds and do what they feel is right, regardless of what sneers follow. One of several children in a fairly well-to-do New England family, Hepburn began her acting career on the stage. In 1932, she was cast in *A Bill of Divorcement* opposite John Barrymore, which prompted her to be cast in several more RKO roles in the 1930s, including the screwball hit *Bringing Up Baby* (1938) with Cary Grant.

Hepburn thrilled audiences in the 1940s with strong performances in *The Philadelphia Story* (1940) and *Woman of the Year* (1942), the film that sparked her most significant relationship—both onscreen and off—with Spencer Tracy. What was not known in the 1940s was that Tracy, Catholic and

Opposite: Paul Newman and Elizabeth Taylor in a volatile scene from *Cat On a Hot Tin Roof* (1958). During the filming, Taylor's husband, Mike Todd, was killed in an airplane crash. Taylor stopped eating. Unbeknownst to Taylor, director Richard Brooks kept calling for take after take of a birthday party scene, in order to force her to eat.

married, lived a double life as Hepburn's lover until his death. The Hepburn-Tracy magic flourished in such films as *Without Love* (1945), *Adam's Rib* (1949), *Pat and Mike* (1952), and *Desk Set* (1957). The last film the pair made together was the classic *Guess Who's Coming to Dinner* in 1967. Hepburn is one of the Academy's most decorated actresses, having been nominated for and won more Oscars than any other performer in Hollywood history. She continued to work well into her senior years in such films as *The Lion In Winter* (1968), the televison film *Love Among The Ruins* (1975), and *On Golden Pond* (1981) with Henry and Jane Fonda.

Although she will probably be best remembered for her role opposite Humphrey Bogart in *Casablanca* (1942), Ingrid Bergman wove a rare and luminous charisma through several memorable roles. A former student at Stockholm's Royal Dramatic Theater School, she left Sweden in the mid-1930s and was quickly signed to a contract with David O. Selznick. Under his direction, she reprised an earlier 1936 Swedish role in a new American version of *Intermezzo* (1939). The remake was both a critical and commercial success.

After Bergman's magnetic performance in *Casablanca*, offers poured in. She received an Oscar nomination for *For Whom the Bell Tolls* (1943) and won for her performance in *Gaslight* (1944). Hitchcock cast her in *Spellbound* (1945) and

Opposite: Humphrey Bogart and Ingrid Bergman together for the immortal *Casablanca* (1942). Bergman has remarked about her performances that "There was often nothing in my face. But the audience put into my face what they thought I was giving."

Notorious (1946). Her passionate portrayal of Saint Joan in *Joan of Arc* (1948) earned her yet another Oscar nomination, although it was overshadowed by damaging notoriety.

Bergman created a scandal when gossip columnists learned that she was involved in an extramarital affair with Italian director Roberto Rossellini and pregnant with his child. Forced to choose between family and Rossellini, and disgraced publicly, she moved in with her lover, who cast her in several films, including *Stromboli* (1950). It took her a long time to find acceptance in Hollywood again. In 1956, she starred in *Anastasia*, which earned her yet another Academy Award. After that performance, however, most of her films were fairly mediocre. She did manage to win a third Oscar for *Murder on the Orient Express* (1974). Her final performance was in the title role of the 1982 TV miniseries *A Woman Called Golda*.

A former model, Lauren Bacall won her first film role opposite Humphrey Bogart in *To Have and Have Not* (1944) after the wife of director Howard Hawks showed her husband Bacall's photo on the cover of a fashion magazine. Nineteen years old, Bacall headed off to Hollywood, where she discovered both fame and a husband. Bogie and Bacall fell in love on the set, and they married in 1945.

The couple appeared together in three other films: *The Big Sleep* (1945), *Dark Passage* (1947), and *Key Largo* (1948). But their magic was not to last. By the late 1950s Bogie was seriously ill, and he died of cancer in 1957. After rumored liasions with Adlai Stevenson and Frank Sinatra, Bacall married Jason Robards in 1961. They divorced in 1969.

Bacall's film roles were scattered and few after Bogie's death, but she did make a comeback in 1974's *Murder on the Orient Express*. She also starred on Broadway in the musical *Applause, Applause* and won a Tony Award in 1970. In recent years, most of her screen roles have been supporting stints. She appeared in *Misery* (1990) as James Caan's literary agent and played Barbra Streisand's domineering mother in *The Mirror Has Two Faces* (1996). Bacall has also done a few made-for-television movies, including the 1999 miniseries *Too Rich: The Secret Life of Doris Duke*.

A New Wave

....

A dedicated actress throughout her high school and college years, Meryl Streep made her first Hollywood appearance in *Julia* (1977). Her powerful performance led her to a larger role in *The Deer Hunter* (1978), which won her an Oscar nomination. In 1979, she made *The Seduction of Joe Tynan*, *Manhattan*, and *Kramer vs. Kramer*. Her earnest child-custody battle with Dustin Hoffman in *Kramer* brought her her first Oscar.

The 1980s afforded Streep more memorable roles, in *Sophie's Choice* (1982), for which she won another Oscar; *The French Lieutenant's Woman* (1981); *Silkwood* (1983); and *Out of Africa* (1985). Unfortunately, most of the films she made in the 1990s were panned as not being up to her usual caliber. If nothing else, these later films display her wide-ranging talents—she plays a romance novelist in *She-Devil* (1989), a reluctantly aging beauty queen in *Death Becomes Her* (1992),

the petulant daughter of a famous overbearing mother in *Postcards From the Edge* (1990), and the dowdy heroine in *The Bridges of Madison County* (1995). In 1996, she appeared with an all-star cast, including Diane Keaton, Leonardo DiCaprio, and Robert De Niro, in *Marvin's Room*. Most recently, she was nominated for Best Actress for her sensitive portrayal of a dying mother in *One True Thing* (1998).

Susan Sarandon's first screen performance, in *Joe* (1970), led to several forgettable films, until she landed a role in the cult classic *The Rocky Horror Picture Show* (1975). She came to more serious notice in director Louis Malle's controversial *Pretty Baby* in 1978. Malle cast her again in *Atlantic City* (1980) opposite Burt Lancaster; this time she captured her first Academy Award nomination. In the 1980s, she appeared in *Loving Couples* (1980), *Compromising Positions* (1985), and *The Witches of Eastwick* (1987). In 1988 she starred opposite Kevin Costner and Tim Robbins in the sexy baseball story *Bull Durham* (1988), for which she received rave reviews.

But the 1990s would prove to be her decade. Sarandon was nominated for an Academy Award for her role as Thelma opposite Geena Davis in *Thelma and Louise* (1991), and again for *Lorenzo's Oil* in 1992. She received her fourth Academy Award nomination for 1994's *The Client* and finally grabbed the statue for 1995's *Dead Man Walking*.

Diane Keaton made her screen debut in 1970 in *Lovers and Other Strangers* and was cast in the phenomenally successful *The Godfather (1972)* as Kay, the hapless wife of mobster Michael Corleone. Keaton reprised her role in that film's two

sequels in 1974 and 1990. But Keaton's innate quirkiness wasn't really acknowledged until she appeared in Woody Allen's *Play It Again, Sam (1972), Sleeper* (1973) and *Love and Death* (1975). Allen's partner both onscreen and off for most of the decade, she reached a memorable peak playing the title role in *Annie Hall* (1977), for which she won an Academy Award. Another critically acclaimed performance followed in Allen's *Manhattan* (1979).

Above: Susan Sarandon in *The Client* (1994), one of many Academy Award–nominated performances that lead to her win for *Dead Man Walking* (1995).

The early 1980s were good for Keaton; she delivered strong performances in *Shoot the Moon* (1982) and *Reds* (1981), for which she received an Academy Award nomination. She followed those with *Crimes of the Heart (1986)*, and *Radio Days* (1987). After playing opposite Steve Martin in the remake of *Father of the Bride (1991)* and its sequel, she took a turn behind the camera, directing the somewhat experimental *Heaven* in 1987. By 1996 she was in front of the cameras again, this time with a meaty role in the critically acclaimed *Marvin's Room* (1996), as well as a more commercial romp in the Paramount hit *The First Wives Club.*

Leading
MEN

Matinee Idols

....

By the time Cary Grant arrived in Hollywood in 1932, he had practically lived another lifetime as Archibald Leach, a runaway who made his living in his native England as an acrobat, juggler, and travelling song-and-dance man. He joined Bob Pender's comedy troupe in 1920, and after a two-year stint, decided to make his home in the United States. In his first film, he was billed as Archie Leach, but after signing with Paramount he became Cary Grant.

Grant's early career was hardly illustrious, although he managed to make a few small films that got him noticed. By the end of 1932, he had appeared in *Blonde Venus* with Marlene Dietrich, one of the studio's biggest stars. He also starred with another bombshell, Mae West, in *She Done Him Wrong* (1933). Several more films followed over the next five

Page 76: Humphrey Bogart was the perfect "tough guy" in such roles as the hard-boiled detective Sam Spade in *The Maltese Falcon* (1941).

Page 77: Dustin Hoffman (left) and Justin Henry in *Kramer vs. Kramer* (1979). Hoffman's immense talent, nurtured by the Method School of Acting, amused Sir Laurence Olivier. On the set of *Marathon Man* (1976), when Hoffman showed up exhausted, Olivier said: "My dear boy, you look absolutely awful. Why don't you try acting? It's so much easier."

Left: The irrepressible Cary Grant (left) clings to Eva Marie Saint in *North By Northwest* (1959). Grant was charming, even about his own legendary reputation: "Everyone wants to be Cary Grant. Even I want to be Cary Grant."

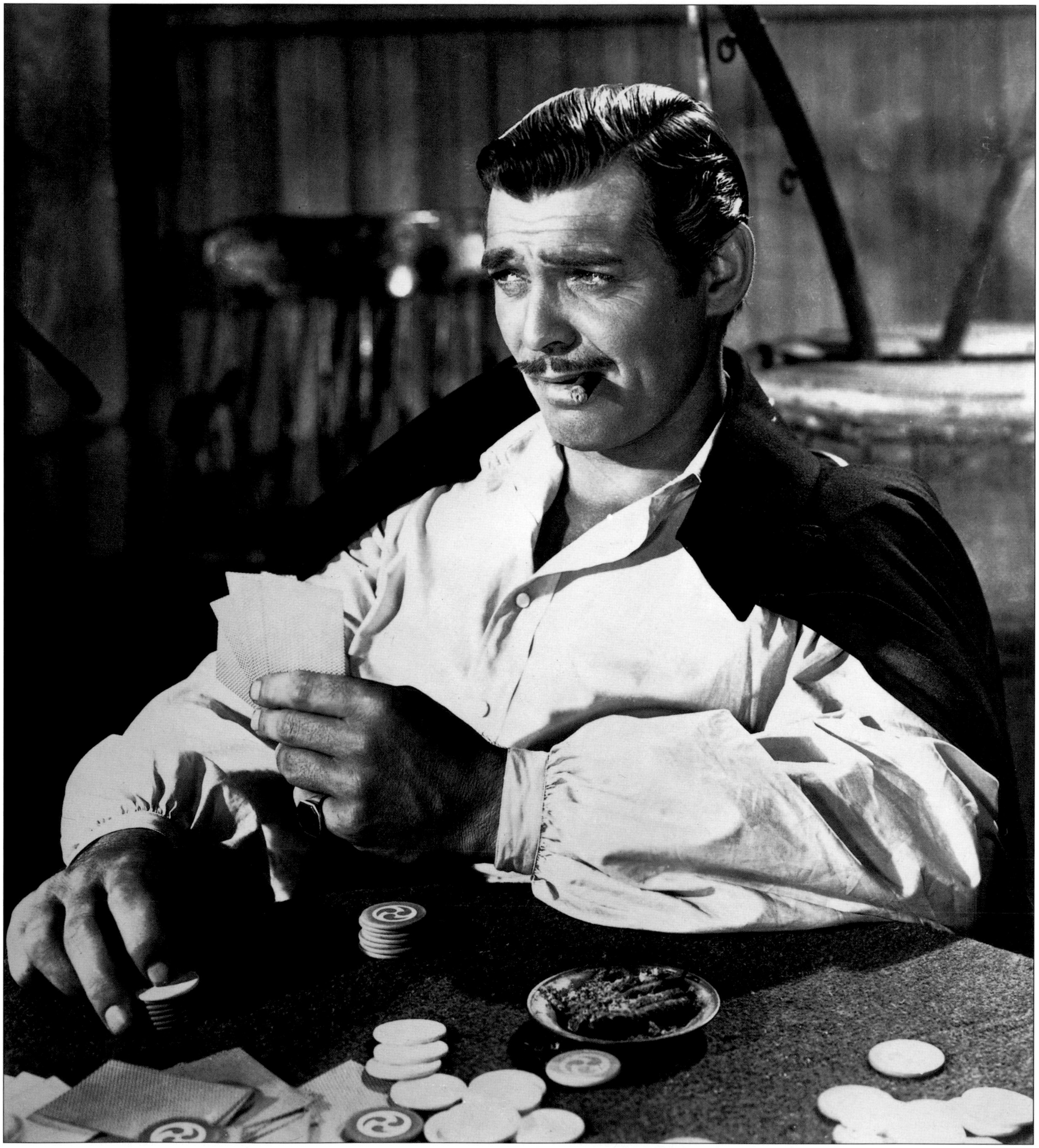

years, in which he developed an impressive talent for the art of the screwball comedy: *Topper* (1937), *The Awful Truth* (1937), *Bringing Up Baby* (1938), *His Girl Friday* (1940), *The Philadelphia Story* (1940), and *My Favorite Wife* (1940).

In 1941 he began a long and successful association with director Alfred Hitchcock, appearing that same year in *Suspicion*, followed by *Notorious* (1944). A decade later, he appeared in *To Catch a Thief* (1955) and *North by Northwest* (1959). Much of the work done for Hitchcock tapped into his particular ability to portray dramatic roles tinged with comedic and urbane sophistication. For the next twenty years, Grant's debonair charm worked its way through almost thirty films. His enormous body of work was finally recognized in 1970, when he was awarded a special Oscar.

The dashing and irresistible Clark Gable became "the king of Hollywood" in the 1930s, owing to his "dangerous" sex appeal, which simmered onscreen opposite some of Hollywood's most devastating female stars, including Greta Garbo, Joan Crawford, Myrna Loy, and Jean Harlow. In 1934, Gable got his first really big break, playing a roguishly head-strong newshound opposite Claudette Colbert's runaway heiress in Frank Capra's *It Happened One Night*. He was hesitant to make the picture, but ultimately trusted Capra and was rewarded. The film raked in the Oscars, with Gable winning Best Actor. Thereafter, he was box office magic.

Under contract, Gable was forced to make several lackluster films that were limited in appeal. Poor quality films continued to dog him throughout the 1940s, even when he was able to exercise a degree of control over them. However, his performance as Fletcher Christian in *Mutiny on the Bounty* (1935) brought him an Oscar nomination, and in 1939 he made film history with his passionate portrayal of Rhett Butler in David O. Selznick's *Gone With the Wind* (1939).

Gable's popularity continued into the 1940s, but tragedy almost ended his career when his wife, actress Carole Lombard, was killed in a plane crash in 1942. Gable took a sabbatical from Hollywood and joined the war effort to deal with his grief. He attempted a comeback in 1945 with *Adventure*, which was a flop. Gable made several more films, throughout the 1940s and 1950s, but his reign as the "king of Hollywood" was at an end. His last film was *The Misfits* (1961).

Paul Newman bristles when anyone mentions his intense blue eyes. However, it is hard to describe his appeal without mentioning them. His chiseled features, coupled with a gracefully aging stage presence, have established him as one of Hollywood's most enduring leading men. He first received notice in *Somebody Up There Likes Me* (1956) and has since captivated audiences with dangerous and brooding roles. Nominated for Academy Awards for such films as *Cat on a Hot Tin Roof* (1958), *The Hustler* (1961), *Hud* (1963), and *Cool Hand Luke* (1967), he was repeatedly passed over. Undeterred, he continued to deliver powerful performances in such films as *Absence of Malice* (1981) and *The Verdict* (1982). After five

Opposite: Clark Gable as the infamous cad Rhett Butler in *Gone With the Wind* (1939). Reportedly, Vivien Leigh was repelled by Gable's bad breath, owing to his less-than-clean false teeth.

unsuccessful nominations, he was awarded an honorary Oscar in 1985. The joke, however, was on the Academy. His next film, *The Color of Money* (1986), finally brought him his first Oscar win.

Newman and his longtime wife, Academy-Award winner Joanne Woodward, have made several films together, from *The Long Hot Summer* (1958) to *Mr. & Mrs. Bridge* (1990). One notable project, *Rachel, Rachel* (1968), directed by Newman and starring Woodward, played to critical acclaim, and Newman was especially lauded for his sensitive direction.

In addition to a successful screen alliance with Joanne Woodward, Paul Newman also enjoyed a special film chemistry with rugged actor Robert Redford. The two were paired together in 1969 for *Butch Cassidy and the Sundance Kid* and then again in 1973 for *The Sting*. Redford received his first Academy Award nomination for the latter.

Beyond playing Paul Newman's sidekick, Redford has achieved his own astounding success. He made his film debut in *War Hunt* (1962), and from there soared into better and better roles. Playwright Neil Simon's *Barefoot in the Park* (1967) launched his stardom and *Butch Cassidy* cemented it. Redford became the male hearthrob of the 1970s. After *The Sting*, he starred in *The Way We Were* (1973), with Barbra Streisand, *Three Days of the Condor* (1975), with Faye Dunaway; and *All the President's Men* (1976), with Dustin

Hoffman. He made his directorial debut in 1980 with *Ordinary People* and won an Academy Award for that effort.

Throughout the 1980s and 1990s, many of Redford's pursuits were directorial, although he accepted roles in such films as *The Natural* (1984), *Out of Africa* (1985), *Havana* (1990), *Sneakers* (1992), and *Indecent Proposal* (1993). Directorial successes from the 1990s include *A River Runs Through It* (1992) and *Quiz Show* (1994), which he also produced. In 1998, *The Horse Whisperer* earned him further accolades. Redford has also worked to develop individual film-makers' talents by establishing the Sundance Film Institute in Utah, which holds an annual independent film festival. The festival has become so successful that winners are assured heavy media attention and plentiful career opportunities.

Rough Around the Edges

Humphrey Bogart's somewhat cynical and world-weary view of life established him as one of Hollywood's favorite stars. He emerged from a well-heeled but troubled childhood with an apparent sense of aimlessness. After joining the Naval Reserve in 1918, he served for one year and then drifted in and out of dead-end jobs, finally discovering a love of acting in 1921 when he played a Japanese butler in a Brooklyn play. Bogart soon conquered Broadway and found his way to Hollywood, at first making bad movies for the Fox Film Corporation. Luckily, his good friend Leslie Howard convinced Warner Brothers to allow Bogie to re-create the role he had mastered on

Opposite: Early in his career Paul Newman tired very quickly of the fuss everyone made over his blue eyes. He scoffed: "Here lies Paul Newman, who died a failure because his eyes turned brown."

Hollywood's
Brightest
Stars

Broadway for the film version of *The Petrified Forest* (1936). Playing opposite stars like James Cagney and Edward G. Robinson in gangster films such as *Angels With Dirty Faces* (1938), Bogart got plenty of attention—but playing a second-banana thug opposite other luminaries was not quite what he had hoped for. Finally, in 1941, Bogie landed the two films that would launch him to stardom: *High Sierra* and *The Maltese Falcon*. A whirlwind of worthy projects followed, including *Casablanca* (1942), for which he earned an Oscar nomination. In 1944, he filmed *To Have and Have Not*, during which he met his fourth wife, Lauren Bacall. The duo's screen chemistry sizzled through three more films.

Bogart's work in the 1950s grew in stature. There was *The African Queen* (1951), for which he earned an Academy Award, *Sabrina* (1954), and *The Caine Mutiny* (1954), for which he won another Oscar nomination. *The Harder They Fall* (1956) was Bogie's last film.

James Cagney, the son of an Irish bartender, was born in New York City, where he grew up on the rough Lower East Side. In the 1920s he toured the country in vaudeville as a song-and-dance man with his wife, Frances, finally ending up on Broadway in a successful musical, *Penny Arcade* (1929). The play brought him out to Hollywood, where he made its film version, entitled *Sinner's Holiday* (1930). However, the vaudevillian repetoire was quickly replaced with a foray into

Opposite: Spencer Tracy, one of Hollywood's consummate actors, relied on simplicity. One of his pieces of advice for novices: "Memorize your lines and don't bump into the furniture."

the disturbed and criminal mind with *Public Enemy* (1931)—the first of several dark and explosive films. As Cagney's stature assumed legendary proportions with *Angels With Dirty Faces* (1938), *The Roaring Twenties* (1939) and *White Heat* (1949), he was increasingly called upon to explore the complex interiors of criminal pathology. Oddly enough, it was Cagney's vaudevillian experience which brought him a Best Actor Academy Award for the musical *Yankee Doodle Dandy* (1942). Other various and successful films included *Mister Roberts* (1955), *Man Of A Thousand Faces* (1957) and *One, Two, Three* (1961). He was coaxed back onto the screen one last time for *Ragtime* (1981), and in 1974 he received the American Film Institute's Life Achievement Award.

At one time, Spencer Tracy considered the priesthood, but while in school, he felt himself drawn to the theater. After studying at the American Academy of Dramatic Arts, he found small parts on Broadway. He never considered a future in the movies until he was signed by John Ford to star in *Up the River* (1930). After that, he set out on a film career, at first in low-budget B-movies, and finally in roles just slightly more worthy of his talent and presence.

Tracy was signed to MGM and played supporting roles in *The Murder Man* (1935) and *Fury* (1936). That same year he earned an Oscar nomination for his role in *San Francisco*. Additional supporting roles followed until he achieved a breakthrough in 1937, when he was cast as a Portuguese fisherman in *Captains Courageous,* opposite child star Freddie Bartholomew. Tracy won the Academy Award and earned yet another the following year for *Boys Town*. By now a legendary star at MGM, Tracy was cast in 1942 opposite Katharine Hepburn in *Woman of the Year*—a project that sparked an affair that would last the rest of his life. Tracy continued to make several films a year, many of them in partnership with Hepburn. Working steadily throughout the 1950s, he displayed wide-ranging skill at both comedy and drama in such diverse films as *Father of the Bride* (1950) with Elizabeth Taylor, which brought him an Academy Award nomination, and *Bad Day at Black Rock* (1955), which led to still another Academy consideration.

By the 1960s, Tracy was tiring, and his projects reflected this, although his performance in 1960's *Inherit the Wind* gained him an Oscar nod. His final film, *Guess Who's Coming to Dinner* (1967), also starred Katharine Hepburn, with Sidney Poitier as the controversial dinner guest. Tracy died three weeks after filming wrapped. Spencer Tracy is remembered for being an actor's actor who believed in hitting his marks, learning his lines, and listening genuinely to his costars' dialogue.

If Dustin Hoffman had begun his career in the 1930s and 1940s, he, like Bogart and Spencer Tracy, probably would have been relegated to B roles until he was able to break out. Luckily, Hoffman's appearance in 1967's acclaimed *The Graduate* launched him to instant stardom—and gained him an Academy Award nomination. But he wouldn't be typecast as a middle-class suburban kid lost in the system in subsequent roles. His portrayal of a street hustler in *Midnight Cowboy* (1969) was nominated for another Academy Award. In *Lenny*

(1974), he played the controversial comedian Lenny Bruce—and received another Oscar nomination. His depiction of Watergate journalist Carl Bernstein in *All the President's Men* (1976) was also well received. He finally won his first Oscar for his role opposite Meryl Streep in 1979's *Kramer vs. Kramer*.

Hoffman has proven consistently that he has a rare and enviable range of talent, playing diverse roles in both comedy and drama with conviction. After playing a divorce-torn father, Hoffman received another Academy Award nomination when he put on a wig and lipstick and masqueraded as a matronly female soap star in the hilarious *Tootsie* (1982). He won an Emmy in 1984 for his interpretation of Willie Loman in the television movie *Death of a Salesman*. After the disastrous *Ishtar* in 1987, Hoffman made a comeback and won yet another Academy Award for his convincing interpretation of an idiot-savant in *Rain Man* (1988). His roles in the 1990s were colorful—a cameo in *Dick Tracy* (1990) and the title role in *Hook* (1991)—and effective—as in *Hero* (1992), *Outbreak* (1995), and *Wag the Dog* (1997).

The Boys Next Door

After spending a couple of years on Broadway, Gregory Peck made his film debut in *Days of Glory* in 1944. His next film, how-

Opposite: Gregory Peck's long and successful career has made him a Hollywood icon. Appearing in a wide variety of roles, his favorite part is that of Atticus Finch, the southern lawyer and widower in *To Kill A Mockingbird* (1962), for which he won an Oscar.

Hollywood's
Brightest
Stars

ever, is the one that made him a star. His role as a Roman Catholic priest in *Keys of the Kingdom* that same year earned him an Academy Award nomination and opened the door for roles in several successful films: *Spellbound* (1944); *The Yearling* (1946), for which he received an Oscar nomination; *Roman Holiday* (1953); and others.

Throughout the 1950s and 1960s, Peck's career soared as he gave memorable performances in *Moby Dick* (1956), *On the Beach* (1959), *The Guns of Navarone* (1961), and *Cape Fear* (1962). His role as southern lawyer Atticus Finch in *To Kill a Mockingbird* (1962) won him his only Oscar. He continued making films throughout the 1960s and 1970s, but slowed down considerably in the 1980s and 1990s. Peck received a Life Achievement Award from the American Film Institute in 1989.

Hollywood's favorite all-American boy, Jimmy Stewart, won the hearts of fans the world over because he was, in truth, every inch the affable, solid citizen he played on screen. Stewart inched his way through numerous insignificant roles during the 1930's before director Frank Capra cast him in *Mr. Smith Goes to Washington* (1939), a blockbuster hit that earned Stewart his first Academy Award nomination. He won his first Oscar for his performance in *The Philadelphia Story* (1940).But is was his role as George Bailey in Frank Capra's *It's a*

Wonderful Life (1946) that proved to be his most memorable. In 1950, Stewart returned to his Broadway roots, starring in the film *Harvey* (based on a Pulitzer Prize–winning play), for which he received another Academy Award nomination.

A handful of Hitchcock classics, including *Rear Window* (1954), the remake of *The Man Who Knew Too Much* (1956), and *Vertigo* (1958) rounded out his career. Stewart died in 1997.

A lifelong friend of Jimmy Stewart, Henry Fonda came across onscreen in much the same way as his lanky pal. He was someone you wanted to know—or figured you already did. It was a persona that served him well in a number of films in a variety of genres, from screwball comedies to westerns. Fonda really came into his own when he hooked up with director John Ford in 1939 to make *Drums Along the Mohawk* (1939) and *The Grapes of Wrath* (1940), the latter earning him an Oscar nomination. Fonda continued a rich relationship with Ford until the two had a falling-out during the filming of *Mister Roberts* in 1955.

In 1957, Fonda starred in and also coproduced the acclaimed *12 Angry Men*. In 1981, he starred with his daughter Jane and Katharine Hepburn in *On Golden Pond*, his last film, for which he won his only Oscar.

Following in the footsteps of Stewart, Peck, and Fonda, Tom Hanks has become the everyman actor for the 1990s. His spontaneous comic style has proven easily adaptable for romances, epics, and dramas. His Oscar-nominated portrayal of a man-child in *Big*, (1988) paved the way for back-to-back Best Actor wins for *Philadelphia* (1993) and *Forrest Gump* (1994).

Femmes Fatales and
SEX SYMBOLS

Foreign Beauties

Born in Sweden in 1905, Greta Garbo arrived in Hollywood in the 1920s, the protégée of director Mauritz Stiller. Louis B. Mayer didn't think much of her. She was plump and introverted, but Stiller made it clear that unless she got a contract with MGM, he wouldn't sign on either. Mayer gave Garbo a $350-per-week deal covering three years and put her to work. During a quick succession of films, Garbo demonstrated her intuitive affinity for the lens and quickly became a star. *Flesh and the Devil* (1927) with John Gilbert gave audiences one of the most torrid onscreen pairings ever—Garbo and Gilbert were very much involved off-screen, too.

Garbo, shrewdly assessing her box-office potential after only one year, confronted Mayer with new salary demands. His mouth fell open when she asked for $5,000 a week. He offered her half, to which she replied, "I tank I go home." That line and the subsequent nine-month strike she staged quickly laid the foundation for her cult status—especially since she won. Mayer finally met her demands, and it is said that over time, he came to enjoy wrangling with her.

In 1930, Garbo made the transition to sound. While MGM producers and audiences held their breath, Garbo assumed the role of a prostitute in the film *Anna Christie* (1930). The first lines she uttered were: "Give me a visky. Ginger ale on the side. And don' be stingy, baby." The voice rolled out like rich butterscotch, and her success was assured. Lavish films followed quickly. *Mata Hari* (1932); *Grand Hotel* (1932), in which Garbo said she "vanted to be alone"; *Queen Christina* (1933), *Anna Karenina* (1935), *Camille* (1936), and finally *Ninotchka* (1939). In 1941, at the age of thirty-six, Garbo walked away from Hollywood. She lived the rest of her life in seclusion in New York City.

Marlene Dietrich is a Hollywood legend, both for her devastating femmes fatales onscreen and her colorful personal life, which involved numerous torrid affairs with both men and women. She made her first appearance in Hollywood in 1923 in *The Little Napoleon*. Throughout the 1920s, she performed regularly, both onstage and in the movies. In 1930, she had her first real break in film when director Josef von Sternberg cast her in *The Blue Angel*.

The pairing proved to be a success, and the two collaborated on several more films, including *Morocco* (1930), *Blonde*

Page 90: A rare full-face peek at Veronica Lake, one of American film noir's great assets, who is usually remembered for the shock of blond hair spilling over one eye.

Page 91: Sex goddess Marilyn Monroe in *The Seven Year Itch* (1955). The film's famous scene in which Monroe's dress billows up to her waist while she cools herself over a subway grate in the sidewalk was witnessed on the set by husband Joe DiMaggio. He was appalled and found the scene humiliating.

Opposite: Greta Garbo—ethereal, luminous, and elusive. She said: "I've always wanted two lives: one for the movies and one for myself." At the top of her game, Garbo walked away from Hollywood without so much as a backward glance.

Venus (1932), and *The Devil Is a Woman* (1935). After the two parted ways during the 1930s, Dietrich continued to make successful films, including *Desire* (1936) and *Destry Rides Again* (1939) with Jimmy Stewart.

In the 1940s, Dietrich starred with onetime romantic inter-est John Wayne in several films, including *Pittsburgh* (1942), which also featured Randolph Scott. When she was sum-moned back to her native Germany by Adolph Hitler to make pro-Nazi films she adamantly refused and—to add insult to injury—entertained Allied troops in Europe with the USO instead. Dietrich began to slow down after World War II, mak-ing fewer and fewer films in the 1950s and 1960s. Her last major role was in *Judgment at Nuremberg* (1961), although she appeared in cameos in two other films, *Paris When It Sizzles* (1964) and *Just a Gigolo* (1979).

Gina Lollobrigida made a splash when she arrived in Hollywood from Italy in the late 1940s, but unfortunately, most of the roles that Hollywood gave her were not designed to encourage her acting talents. She made her debut in 1954 in John Huston's *Beat the Devil* and subsequently starred opposite some of Hollywood's most exciting leading men, including Anthony Quinn in *The Hunchback of Notre Dame* (1957) and Rock Hudson in *Come September* (1961). She left Hollywood in the mid-1970s, but appeared in a couple of TV dramas during the 1980s.

Left: Marlene Dietrich's enigmatic qualities were summed up by critic Kenneth Tynan, who said her "masculinity appeals to women, and her sexuality to men."

For Sophia Loren, fame came in the 1950s, notably with *Boy on a Dolphin* (1957), which was immediately followed by *The Pride and the Passion* (1957). While she established her career in Hollywood first, it was in Italian films that the Loren magic completely emerged, as it did in *Two Women* (1961). Loren won an Oscar for her wrenching performance.

Her comedic talents were considerable as well. In the 1960s, Loren created cherished film moments in *Yesterday, Today and Tomorrow* (1963) and *Marriage Italian-Style* (1964). Loren made history in *Yesterday* with a steamy striptease played to costar Marcello Mastroianni.

Her career thrived despite numerous personal problems. At the beginning of her career she fell in love with producer Carlo Ponti, who wanted to marry her despite a large age difference. Soon after, on the set of *The Pride And The Passion* (1957), Loren fell under the irresistible spell of Cary Grant. They had a well publicized affair and Grant also proposed marriage. Loren was badly torn. She decided she had a better chance at a successful partnership with Ponti, a fellow Italian with similar sensibilities. However, following her Mexican marriage to Ponti, charges of bigamy were leveled against the couple by the Italian government, because it did not recognize Ponti's earlier divorce. Loren also experienced miscarriages and two difficult pregnancies, and even served a jail term for tax evasion. Her film career slumped somewhat in the 1970s and 1980s but has resumed with sparkle in recent years with Robert Altman's *Prêt-à-Porter* (aka *Ready to Wear*, 1994) and *Grumpier Old Men* (1995).

Busting Out

Voted at one time the most beautiful woman in the world, Ava Gardner is perhaps more famous for her great beauty—and her tempestuous romance with Frank Sinatra—than for her acting. The gorgeous southern belle came onto the Hollywood scene in the early 1940s, playing mostly B parts until she was signed to *The Killers* in 1946. Her success in that film got her a singing role opposite Clark Gable in *The Hucksters* (1947), which led to more singing in 1951's *Show Boat*. Gardner reunited with Gable in 1953's *Mogambo* and found her role of a lifetime in *The Barefoot Contessa* (1954). She made several more films in the 1960s through the 1980s, and even appeared on television in the primetime soap *Falcon Crest* for a season in 1985.

Betty Grable made her first film appearance at fourteen in *Whoopee!* (1930). Throughout the early 1930s she had insignificant roles in equally insignificant films until she was cast in *The Gay Divorcee* (1934) with Fred Astaire and Ginger Rogers. She made several more films in the 1930s, both musical and dramatic. In 1940, her break came playing the lead in the musical *Down Argentine Way*. Many other starring roles were to follow.

Throughout World War II, Betty Grable's legs boosted American GI's morale as much as thoughts of Christmas back home. Hers was the number-one pinup of homesick soldiers overseas. Fox insured her legs for a million dollars. In addition to beauty, talent, and charm, Grable was a symbol of American wholesomeness.

Raquel Welch was by no means an overnight success. A former pageant winner, she had small parts in a few films in the mid-1960s and supplemented her income by modeling, which proved to be more lucrative and was what finally got her noticed. In 1966, she had two breaks: the sci-fi adventure film *Fantastic Voyage* and *One Million Years B.C.*, but she was always more of a bombshell than a serious actress. In 1967, she starred in *Bedazzled* with Dudley Moore and Peter Cook, and then played opposite Frank Sinatra in *Lady in Cement* (1968). She made a few films during the 1970s, and in the 1980s, she assumed the lead in the Broadway musical *Woman of the Year*.

Blonde Bombshells

Jean Harlow's platinum tresses touched off a nationwide fashion craze, while her private life sparked constant speculation and high interest. An accomplished comedienne, Harlow had the good fortune to be given scripts that demanded tough, wisecracking dialogue, and she traded zingy one-liners with such famous partners as Clark Gable, Spencer Tracy, and William Powell.

Right: Actress Raquel Welch spent a fortune promoting her physical attributes and finally got noticed. Not happy with her sex symbol image, she tried to further a serious acting career. It went nowhere.

Harlow's rise began in 1930 with her appearance in RKO's *Hell's Angels*. Quickly establishing herself as a money-maker, she moved to MGM in 1932. Her major films include *Platinum Blonde* (1931), *Red-Headed Woman* (1932), *Bombshell* (1933), *Hold Your Man* (1933), *Dinner at Eight* (1933), *China Seas* (1935), and *Libeled Lady* (1936). According to various accounts, Harlow turned down a marriage proposal from William Powell, accepting MGM executive Paul Bern's, instead. The 1932 liaison proved fatal. After a disastrous two-month marriage, Harrow quietly separated from Bern, who later committed suicide.

News of Bern's suicide note and its contents added even more speculation to the scandal. There were rumors that Harlow was beaten viciously as well as of Bern's impotence. Harlow died at age twenty-six of uremia, shortly after filming *Saratoga* (1937). While this allegation has never been confirmed, her onetime agent insisted that her kidney failure was caused by injuries sustained from a particularly vicious fight with Bern, which had been hushed up. More recent accounts state that Harlow suffered from incurable kidney disease. Regardless, Harlow's mother, a Christian Scientist, blocked the offer of medical intervention for her daughter from Louis B. Mayer's physician.

Often referred to as another Monroe wannabe, Jayne Mansfield had a chest that swelled larger than Marilyn's, but the same cannot be said of her career. One film, *Will Success Spoil Rock Hunter?* (1957), was highly rated—not so much for Mansfield's performance as for its clever satirical script. A variety of publicity stunts and assorted plunging necklines kept Mansfield on the front pages, but her career went nowhere. She died in an auto accident in 1967.

Veronica Lake is probably most famous for her sweeping blond hairdo—copied by Kim Basinger for her role as a 1940s prostitute in 1997's *L.A. Confidential*. Lake's career lasted little more than a decade, but the impact she left is timeless. Her fist big role was opposite Joel McCrea in *Sullivan's Travels* (1941), and her success led her to an on-screen partnership with Alan Ladd in such films as *This Gun for Hire* (1942), *The Glass Key* (1942), and *The Blue Dahlia* (1946). Sadly, her career did not have the necessary momentum to carry her into the next decade. Her last appearance onscreen was in *Stronghold* in 1951.

Lana Turner, the "sweater girl," was supposedly discovered across the counter at an ice-cream shop in Los Angeles in the late 1930s. She didn't achieve star status, however, until 1941, when she made four films: *Ziegfeld Girl*, *Dr. Jekyll and Mr. Hyde*, *Honky Tonk*, and *Johnny Eager*. Several fine performances followed, in films including *The Postman Always Rings Twice* (1946) and *The Three Musketeers* (1948). In the 1950s and 1960s, she starred in several films that got mixed reviews and finally received an Academy Award nomination for her role in *Peyton Place* (1957). Most of her later work was in television.

Opposite: The "Blonde Bombshell" Jean Harlow was the bias-cut gown's best promoter. Her wise-cracking dialogue and sexual allure vaulted her to stardom.

Sexpot Legends

One of Hollywood's hot blond "mamas," Mae West was a former vaudevillian and stage actress who was forty years old when she first appeared on screen—and who had young men living with her well into her seventies. Her specialty was sex, her weapon, dialogue, and her target, middle-class morality. In fact, her brand of comedy was so uniquely naughty, it became legendary.

West wrote her own material—plays and sketches riddled with one-liners that still zing today. Whereas other women played the game out of necessity, as a means to a respectable end, West seemed more interested in physical pleasure for its own sake. "Like I always say," she murmured, "it's not the men in your life, it's the life in your men."

In 1933, West brought her play *Diamond Lil* to the screen, retitled *She Done Him Wrong*; she costarred in it with Cary Grant. In 1940, she exchanged one-liners with W.C. Fields in *My Little Chickadee*. Some of the best-remembered Mae West lines include: "Is that a gun you're carrying in your pocket or are you just glad to see me?"; "I used to be Snow White, but I drifted"; and "Give a man a free hand and he'll run it all over you."

West's talent might have eventually melted into the Hollywood pot of has-beens were it not for a second career launch in the 1960s, sparked by the new feminist movement. Young women, discovering her work in films, suddenly found a new role model. Here was an accomplished writer and comedi-enne who had struck out on her own with an open and refreshing sexuality. For those young impressionable film buffs, Mae West opened different doors to self-expression and freedom.

In the 1950s and early 1960s, Marilyn Monroe dominated men's fantasies with her blond hair, come-hither half smile, and curvaceous hips. Monroe played a variety of roles ranging from a disturbed babysitter in *Don't Bother to Knock* (1952) to the loveable and ditzy Sugar in *Some Like It Hot* (1959). Onscreen, Monroe was by turns confused, troubled, kittenish, or sweetly sexy. Some of her most successful films include *Niagara* (1953), *Gentlemen Prefer Blondes* (1953), *How to Marry a Millionaire* (1953), and *The Seven Year Itch* (1955). Her last film was *The Misfits* in 1961.

Monroe had posed nude as a calendar pinup in 1949, earning the grand sum of $50—and millions of adorers. Her career finally launched, she made headlines almost daily as her personal life assumed melodramatic proportions. There was a whirlwind courtship and marriage to legendary American baseball player Joe DiMaggio, followed by a disastrous marriage to playwright Arthur Miller. On August 5, 1962, Monroe was found dead, from an overdose of sleeping pills. Since then, colleagues, gossips, and writers have spun numerous theories about her death, ranging from a suicide to a government murder conspiracy.

Mae West, shrewd and independent, wrote most of her own comic material, peppering it with sexual innuendo. Feminists of the 1960s re-discovered her early films and elevated her to cult status.

The Good,
the Bad, and
THE ACTION HERO

Westerns and More

Throughout a career that spanned more than 250 films, John Wayne was the all-American hero. Strong, silent, terse, crusty, and principled, he was the anti-Communist ideal.

Born Marion Michael Morrison, John Wayne was the father of the action hero, as well as the embodiment of righteousness and values in the twentieth-century male. But Wayne almost never made it to films. He played small, mediocre parts in many silent films, which went practically unnoticed. But he established a friendship with director John Ford. Ford saw Wayne's potential and recommended him for a screen test for *The Big Trail* (1930). It might have meant Wayne's big break, but the film flopped miserably.

After that debacle, Wayne signed with Warner, making low-budget films throughout the 1930s, stuck in westerns and B-movies. It wasn't until his old pal John Ford called him in to test for *Stagecoach* (1939) that Wayne's career really got underway. In the early 1940s, he left the Bs behind and played opposite such screen goddesses as Marlene Dietrich in *Pittsburgh* (1942), Joan Crawford in *Reunion in France* (1942), and Claudette Colbert in *Without Reservations* (1946). He won critical acclaim for his performances in *Red River* and *Fort Apache*, both in 1948.

In the early 1950s, he teamed up with Maureen O'Hara for *Rio Grande* (1950) and *The Quiet Man* (1952). Also at that time, Wayne coproduced and starred in *Big Jim McLain* (1952) and

The High and the Mighty (1954), among others. He reunited with John Ford in 1956 for *The Searchers*. The 1960s also saw some of Wayne's best-remembered westerns, including *The Alamo* (1960), *The Man Who Shot Liberty Valance* (1962)—with Jimmy Stewart—and *True Grit* (1969). In 1975, he made the sequel to *True Grit*, *Rooster Cogburn*, with fellow screen legend Katharine Hepburn. Wayne's last film, *The Shootist* (1976), also starred Jimmy Stewart. Wayne died of cancer in 1979.

Like so many other actors of his era, Gary Cooper started his film career as an extra in silent films in the 1920s. By the middle of that decade, he became a face moviegoers started to recognize. Although he had his first big part in *The Winning of Barbara Worth* (1926) and was featured in Clara Bow's legendary *It* (1927), it was westerns that put food on his table in the late 1920s. In the next decade, he would break out of that stereotype, costarring with Marlene Dietrich in *Morocco* (1930) and in Frank Capra's *Mr. Deeds Goes to Town* in 1936. It was for this film that Cooper won his first Oscar nomination.

Page 102: James Dean, the new anti-hero of the fifties, was moody, violent, and troubled. On September 30, 1955, he was killed in a car accident. Both *Rebel Without a Cause* (1955) and *Giant* (1956) were released after his death and he achieved cult status by the 1960s.

Page 103: Jack Nicholson in *The Passenger* (1975). Nicholson's roles over the years have included many violent, brooding, or rebellious characters, but he is equally gifted in comedy.

Opposite: Gary Cooper, circa 1938. Cooper remains a legendary figure on the American landscape having glamorized the image of the average man. Critics feel he gave his finest performance in *High Noon* (1952).

Hollywood's
Brightest
Stars

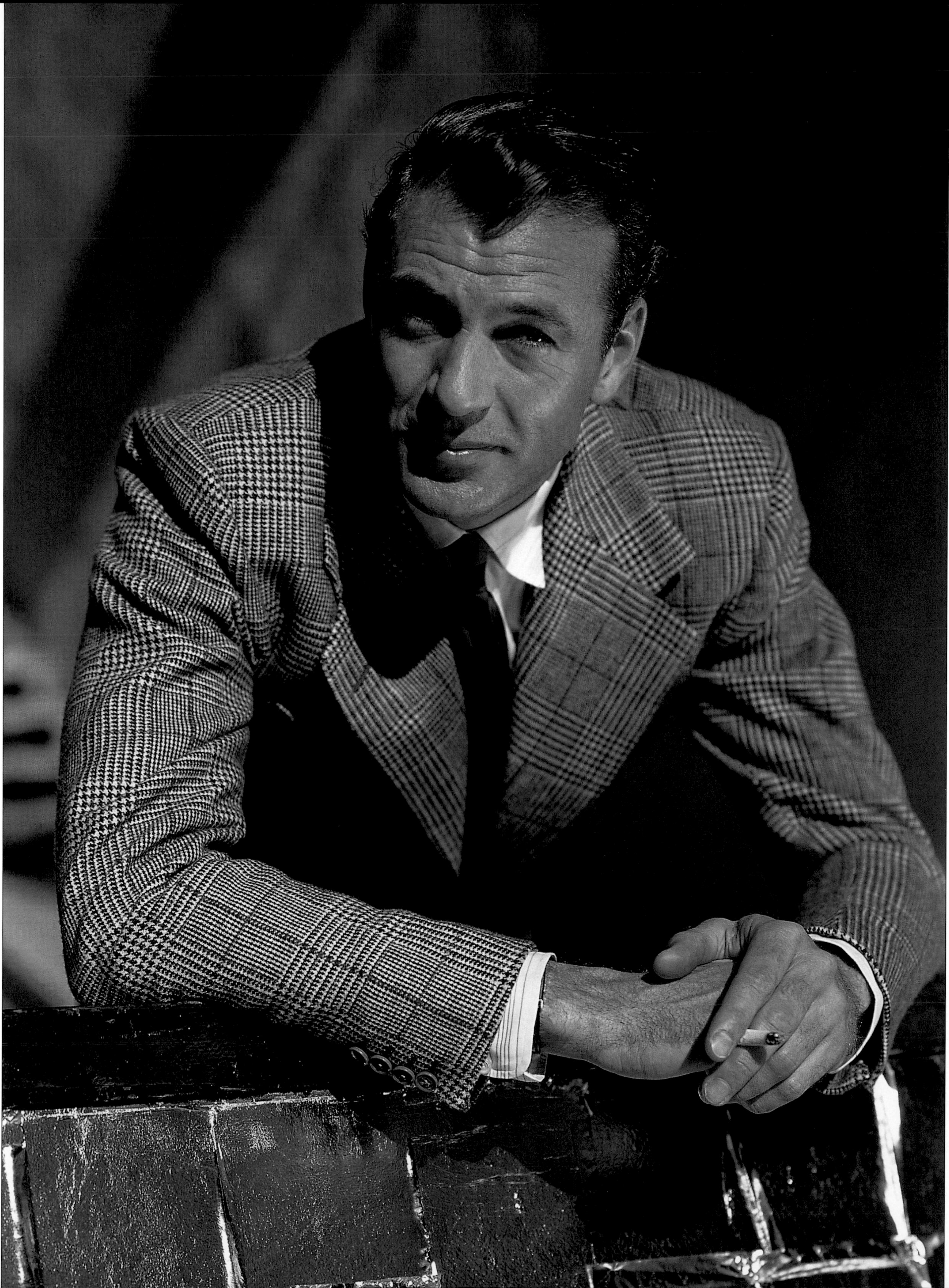

The 1940s proved to be a mixed bag of laughs, tears, and celebrated performances. Cooper teamed up with Frank Capra again for *Meet John Doe* in 1941. That same year, he starred in *Sergeant York*, winning his first Academy Award for Best Actor. His portrayal of baseball great Lou Gehrig in *The Pride of the Yankees* (1942) got him another Oscar nod. In 1952, Cooper was cast opposite ingenue Grace Kelly for *High Noon*—his last Oscar-winning performance. *Love in the Afternoon* (1957) with Audrey Hepburn was one of his last performances, as his career did not reach very far into the next decade. He won a special Academy Award in 1961 and died in May of that same year.

Short of stature but long on screen presence, the five-foot, five-inch (1.6m) Alan Ladd had his first major role in *This Gun for Hire* in 1942. Aside from his work in westerns, he was frequently teamed with Veronica Lake in the 1940s and made lots of war dramas and crime films. Unlike Lake, Ladd was able to carry his career into the next decade—but not long into it. In 1953, he was cast in the starring role in *Shane*. The incredible success of this western was no match for Ladd's personal demons, however; he died of a drug overdose shortly after making *The Carpetbaggers* (1964).

Clint Eastwood became a star almost by accident. Although he had big dreams when he came to Hollywood in 1955, he was unable to break into movies, and turned to tele-

vision. In 1959, he landed a role in *Rawhide*. After *Rawhide* successfully played itself out, Eastwood went to Italy to make a series of what would be known as "spaghetti westerns." On the huge success of *A Fistful of Dollars* (1964), he returned to Italy to make *For a Few Dollars More* (1966) and *The Good, the Bad and The Ugly* (1966).

Eastwood was finally recognized in the late 1960s, and despite the disastrous musical *Paint Your Wagon* (1969), he was well on his way to stardom, with such films as *Coogan's Bluff* (1968). In 1972, Eastwood appeared as Dirty Harry in the original *Dirty Harry*. Interestingly, Eastwood got this career-defining role only after Frank Sinatra dropped out. In 1971, Eastwood starred in *Play Misty for Me*, demonstrating a talent that surpassed westerns and cop films.

In the 1970s, Eastwood founded Malapaso, his own production company, which turned out hit after hit, including *The Outlaw—Josey Wales* (1976), *Every Which Way But Loose* (1978), and *Escape from Alcatraz* (1979). He changed gears in the early 1990s, taking a seat behind the camera. The result was phenomenal. *Unforgiven* (1992), directed by and starring Eastwood, took home Academy Awards for Best Picture and Best Director. Another directorial success, *The Bridges of Madison County* (1995), also featured Eastwood in a starring role, this time opposite Meryl Streep. Not all of his directorial efforts have been as well received, however; he garnered more than his share of criticism for *Midnight in the Garden of Good and Evil* (1997)—although reviews were favorable for the cast, which included Kevin Spacey.

Opposite: As good playing a cop as he is a cowboy, Clint Eastwood reached Hollywood stardom through television and spaghetti westerns. Director Don Siegel once said of Clint: "Hardest thing in the world is to do nothing, and he does it marvelously."

Action Heros

Steve McQueen is to action heroes what Cary Grant is to matinee idols. The blue-eyed, blond-haired survivor of a troubled childhood got his start on Broadway and found his way to Hollywood in the mid-1950s. He appeared in *Somebody Up There Likes Me* (1956), but he did not have his first starring role until the campy classic *The Blob* (1958).

McQueen acted in numerous films during the twenty-some odd years he spent in Hollywood, most of which showcased his tough-guy coolness: *The Magnificent Seven* (1960), *The Great Escape* (1963), *Bullitt* (1968), *The Getaway* (1972),

Papillon (1973), and *The Hunter* (1980). McQueen died of a heart attack after cancer surgery in 1980, but his legacy lives on.

Raised in the Bahamas in utter poverty, Sidney Poitier finished only a few years of formal education before enlisting in the army. After he served his term, he headed for Broadway, where he was able to find a few good roles. From there he moved on to Hollywood and a part in *No Way Out* (1950). Several minor roles followed, until he broke through in compelling films, playing a rebellious student in *Blackboard Jungle* (1955) and a dock worker in 1957's *Edge of the City*.

Poitier received an Oscar nomination for *The Defiant Ones* (1958) and truly established himself as a leading man. Several successful films followed, but only one brought him an Oscar win—*Lilies of the Field* (1963). His powerful onscreen presence as a dignified success symbol of the civil rights movement brought him memorable roles in such films as *Guess Who's Coming to Dinner, To Sir, With Love,* and *In the Heat of the Night*—all released in 1967. In 1968, he wrote and starred in *For Love of Ivy*, and in 1972, he directed and starred in *Buck and the Preacher*.

Left: Sidney Poitier (left) and Rod Steiger in *The Heat of the Night* (1967), the winner of five Oscars.

Opposite: Action hero Steve McQueen made a short but dazzling list of performances in such films as *The Great Escape* (1963), *The Sand Pebbles* (1966), *The Thomas Crown Affair* (1968), *Bullitt* (1968), and *Papillon* (1973), before his premature death in 1980.

By the 1980s, Poitier had given up acting to concentrate on directing such films as *Stir Crazy* (1980) and *Hanky Panky* (1982). Poitier resumed his place in front of the camera for a few roles, including a powerful portrayal of Supreme Court Justice Thurgood Marshall in the made-for-television movie *Separate but Equal* (1991).

Scottish actor Sean Connery was writer Ian Fleming's Secret Agent 007—and then some. He made his film debut in 1954 in *Lilacs in the Spring*. In 1962, he gained notice in *The Longest Day*, and later that year he became the original—and quite possibly the best—Bond, James Bond, in *Dr. No*. Other successful Bond flicks of that era include *From Russia With Love* (1963), *Goldfinger* (1964), *Thunderball* (1965), *You Only Live Twice* (1967), and *Diamonds Are Forever* (1971). Connery made a break from his world-famous character to try other parts in the 1960s and 1970s, but could not seem to shake the 007 image. He gave audiences what they wanted and revived his famous character in *Never Say Never Again* (1983).

In addition to his Bond roles, Connery created a new identity for himself in the *Highlander* films. He was named Best Supporting Actor in 1987 for his performance in *The Untouchables*. In 1989, Connery played the father of another famed action hero, teaming up with Harrison Ford in *Indiana Jones and the Last Crusade*. Every inch a senior sex symbol,

Opposite: Sean Connery and Ursula Andress in *Dr. No* (1962). At one point in his career Connery barked: "I've always hated that damn James Bond. I'd like to kill him."

Connery has also given strong performances in *The Hunt for Red October* (1990), *Rising Sun,* (1993) and *The Rock* (1996); however, his performance in the romantic comedy *Playing By Heart* (1999) was not as successful.

Harrison Ford may have found both fame and fortune for his portrayals of Han Solo and Indiana Jones, but the actor has a range that encompasses everything from action hero to comedian to serious dramatist. Although Ford had his first featured role in *American Graffiti* (1973), it wasn't until 1977 that his career really took off, in the phenomenally successful *Star Wars*. Ford revived that role in subsequent sequels, *The Empire Strikes Back* and *Return of the Jedi*, and in between, he worked on other blockbuster projects.

In 1981, Ford introduced another hero, archaeologist-adventurer Indiana Jones, in *Raiders of the Lost Ark* (1981). Reprising this role in the two *Indiana Jones* sequels, he again demonstrated that good luck comes in threes. Ford also took on another kind of action movie, the dark futuristic sort, with *Blade Runner* in 1982. A mixed bag of films was to follow, including *Witness* (1985), *The Mosquito Coast* (1986), *Frantic* (1988), *Working Girl* (1988), *Presumed Innocent* (1990), *Regarding Henry* (1991), *The Fugitive* (1993), and *Clear and Present Danger* (1994). More recently, he has played romantic leads in the remake of *Sabrina* (1995) as well as *Six Days, Seven Nights* (1998).

Originally from New York State, Australian-bred actor Mel Gibson made his first big film, *Tim* (1979), "down under" and won the Australian equivalent of the Oscar for his performance. He became everyone's favorite post-apocalypse action hero in *Mad Max* (1979), a low-budget sci-fi adventure that spawned the sequels *The Road Warrior* in 1981 and *Mad Max Beyond Thunderdome* in 1985. In *The Year of Living Dangerously* (1983), Gibson broke away from his Mad Max persona. He also made a departure from his typical roles by playing Hamlet in the film version released in 1990. But perhaps the most successful films of his career have been those of the *Lethal Weapon* series, the first movie released in 1987, the second in 1989, the third in 1992, and the fourth in 1998. His initial pairing with Danny Glover and the subsequent additions of Joe Pesci, Rene Russo, and Chris Rock have brought the series an unprecedented following.

Gibson made his directorial debut with *The Man without a Face* in 1993, then went on to direct, produce, and star in the acclaimed epic film *Braveheart* (1995), which garnered a number of Oscars, including Best Picture and Best Director.

The Rebels

Like many of his generation, Marlon Brando made his debut on Broadway, with memorable performances in *I Remember Mama* (1944) and *A Streetcar Named Desire* (1947). But he soon grew too big for the stage and ventured off to Hollywood. His first film was *The Men* (1950). In 1951, he recreated his Stanley Kowalski role in the film version of *Streetcar* with Vivien Leigh. His explosive performance won him an Oscar nomination and icon status. He would be nominated for three more in a row, *Viva Zapata!* (1952), *Julius Caesar* (1953), and *On the Waterfront* (1954); the last earned him the statuette.

In 1955's *Guys and Dolls* (also starring Frank Sinatra), Brando experimented with musicals and comedies with dismaying results. He returned to dramatic roles in such films as *Sayonara* (1957), which gained him another Oscar nomination. He also worked behind the camera for the first time with *One-Eyed Jacks* (1961).

Another role that created film history was Brando's interpretation of the aging Vito Corleone in *The Godfather* (1972). The film was both a critical and box-office success, launching the careers of several actors and earning Brando another Oscar. In 1973, he turned up the sexual heat in Bernardo Bertolucci's highly provocative *Last Tango in Paris*, receiving yet another Oscar nomination. His performance in 1979's *Apocalypse Now* was also well received. In the 1980s, he was nominated again for *A Dry White Season* (1989). His career continued to flourish, though his eccentric lifestyle, problems with his troubled children, and an apparent ambivalence about acting have for the most part kept him off the screen. One of his more recent films, *Don Juan DeMarco* (1995), also starred Faye Dunaway and Johnny Depp.

Opposite: Marlon Brando exploded onto the screen in the 1950s. Of his Oscar-winning performance in *On the Waterfront* (1954), Brando recalls: "On the day Kazan showed me the completed picture I was so depressed by my performance that I got up and left the screening room."

Hollywood's Brightest Stars

While Brando was already an established screen legend when he appeared in *The Godfather*, Al Pacino was a virtual unknown, playing Corleone's morally conflicted son, Michael. This charismatic blend of compelling character and dynamic actor brought Pacino his first Oscar nomination. In 1974, Pacino was nominated again for *The Godfather Part II*. Pacino created other memorable characters in such films as *Serpico* (1973), *Dog Day Afternoon* (1975), and *...And Justice for All* (1979). The latter earned another Oscar nomination.

In 1983, Pacino terrified audiences with a violent rendering of a sleazy mobster in *Scarface*. He then moved to the other side of the law and played a cop in the thriller, *Sea of Love* (1989). His stand-out performance in a colorful role in *Dick Tracy* (1990) earned him a Best Supporting Actor nomination. Next, Pacino demonstrated a sensitive, romantic nature opposite Michelle Pfeiffer in *Frankie and Johnny* (1991). The following year, he was nominated for yet another Academy Award for *Glengarry Glen Ross*. Finally, Pacino won his first Oscar for 1992's *Scent of a Woman*.

Another alumnus of the *Godfather* school of acting, Robert De Niro won Best Supporting Actor for his role as the young Vito Corleone in *The Godfather Part II* (1974). Like so many before him, De Niro began his career off Broadway and in low-budget films. Ultimately, he was cast in *Bang the Drum Slowly* (1973) and *Mean Streets* (1973). *Taxi Driver* (1976)

Opposite: Robert DeNiro beefed himself up considerably for the part of boxer Jake LaMotta in *Raging Bull* (1980). This "meatier" role earned him an Academy Award.

presented him with one of his most frightening roles to date, and the immortal catch-phrase, "Are you talkin' to me?"

Like Brando, De Niro took a stab at musicals with *New York, New York* (1977), costarring Liza Minnelli; he had as much success in that genre as Brando did. Another Oscar nomination was right around the corner, however, with 1978's *The Deerhunter*. He was nominated again—and won—for his performance in *Raging Bull* (1980).

De Niro has played other extraordinary characters in addition to tough guys and mobsters. Although brilliant in 1987's *The Untouchables* and 1990's *Goodfellas*, he also gave convincing performances in *The King of Comedy* (1983); *Midnight Run* (1988), with Charles Grodin; and *We're No Angels* (1989), with Sean Penn. He was nominated again for *Cape Fear* (1991). *A Bronx Tale* (1993) marked his directorial debut.

Writer-producer-director-actor Jack Nicholson made his first appearance onscreen in Roger Corman's *The Cry Baby Killer* (1958). After that, he spent most of his time behind the camera, writing screenplays and producing. He cowrote, coproduced, and made a cameo appearance in the 1968 cult classic *Head*. He received his first Oscar nomination for his role in *Easy Rider* (1969), and stayed in front of the camera consistently over the ensuing decades. In *On a Clear Day You Can See Forever* (1970), he serenaded Barbra Streisand. He also sang in *Tommy* (1975). Tackling meatier roles, he received another Oscar nomination for *Five Easy Pieces* (1970). In *Carnal Knowledge* (1971), he explored sexual mores with Art Garfunkel, Candice Bergen, and Ann-Margret.

Nicholson is one of Hollywood's most frequently nominated actors. Films for which he has received recognition include *The Last Detail* (1973), *Chinatown* (1974), *One Flew Over the Cuckoo's Nest* (1975, a win), *Reds* (1981), 1983's *Terms of Endearment* (another win), *The Witches of Eastwick* (1987), and *A Few Good Men* (1992). He has thrilled audiences with his roles in *The Shining* (1980), *The Postman Always Rings Twice* (1981), and as The Joker in *Batman* (1989). He won his third Academy Award for *As Good as It Gets* (1998).

Muscle Men
··

Sylvester Stallone's career as a super-muscled, bare-chested killing machine soared through the 1980s. He made his mark in *Rocky* (1976), which he also wrote, about a lovable two-bit fighter who gets a shot at the big time and regains his dignity in the bargain. It earned Stallone two nominations, for Best Actor and Original Screenplay, and brought home the Best Picture Oscar. Stallone literally pumped up harder, moving from *Rocky* sequels to *Rambo* sequels, grunting and grimacing his way to historic riches.

Austrian strongman Arnold Schwarzenegger is not your run-of-the-mill Hollywood star. With a name and an accent that were most Hollywood un-friendly, he was largely perceived as more muscle than talent. Yet he rose quickly to stardom, due to his incredible physique as a champion body builder and undeniable screen presence.

After *Stay Hungry* (1976) and *Pumping Iron* (1977), filmmakers saw that he possessed a certain drive and charm that translated well to the screen. In 1982, his accented English and enormous body lent themselves well to *Conan The Barbarian*, and the tremendous hype surrounding the film brought him international attention. A breakthrough in his career occurred in 1984 with *The Terminator*, a critically acclaimed blockbuster in which he played a violent cyborg (humanlike robot), who is unassailable. But Schwarzenegger wanted to reach past the enclave of action-adventure fans. He eventually did so by appearing with Danny DeVito in the lighthearted comedy *Twins* (1988). Audiences also appreciated his mix of brawn, humor, and tenderness in *Kindergarten Cop* (1990).

Responding to what appeared to be kinder, gentler times, Schwarzenegger made *Terminator 2: Judgment Day* (1991), this time playing a heroic cyborg. The film was highly successful. Next, Schwarzenegger made *Last Action Hero* (1993)—a flop, owing to a bad plot and a disagreeable point of view. He sprang back with *True Lies* (1994), a tight mix of action, humor, romance, and incredible special effects. He teamed up again with Danny DeVito and played a pregnant man in *Junior* (1994). Subsequently, he played a crazed gift-buying dad in *Jingle All the Way* (1996).

Opposite: Sylvester Stallone as Rocky Balboa in the Academy-Award winning *Rocky* (1976), which Stallone scripted. "People don't credit me with much of a brain," he said of his win, "so why should I disillusion them?"

Make Me
LAUGH

Classic Teams

The early Depression years were good for the Marx Brothers' brand of comedy—social insanity. Like Mae West, the Marx Brothers employed a mixture of verbal and physical styles that captured comedic perfection in both sight and sound. The Brothers' move into film followed successful careers on Broadway and in radio. Over time, they had come to perfect their personas. Groucho, Chico, and Harpo instigated most of the mayhem, with brother Zeppo adding an occasional touch of the handsome subordinate.

In their early films, *The Cocoanuts* (1929), *Animal Crackers* (1930), *Monkey Business* (1931), and *Horse Feathers* (1932), their assigned roles varied, but their characters remained intact. Harpo was the mute mischief-maker and hopeless romantic; Groucho was the instigator, the wit, the social climber; and Chico was the "ethnic" Italian, clever, scheming, and single-minded. Together, they could turn dinner parties upside down, transform ocean liners into floating circuses, or make democracies into anarchies.

The Marx Brothers left Paramount for Irving Thalberg at MGM, and with his input, they made *A Night At The Opera* (1935), an integration of their brand of humor with Thalberg's intuitive sense of the nation's mood. This film connected with audiences. By the early 1940s, the brothers had split up, only to reunite later that decade for *A Night in Casablanca* (1946) and *Love Happy* (1949).

Stan Laurel and Oliver Hardy were the premiere comedy duo of the century. They made more than thirty films together, starting with the silent screen and moving into the Golden Age. As different as they were, both in stature and background, they had an onscreen chemistry that was pure magic.

Laurel was born in England and came to the United States when film was in its infancy. He toured the vaudeville circuit. Hardy started his career in show business singing in Georgia, making the leap into silents at the same time Laurel was performing in vaudeville. The team first appeared together in *Putting Pants on Philip* (1927), and the rest was history. They easily made the transition to talkies with *Men O' War*, *Perfect Day*, and *The Hoose-Gow* (all in 1929) and achieved an international stardom that carried them through the 1930s and into the next decade. By the mid-1940s, however, the partnership dissolved due to contractual disputes and diminishing success.

Bud Abbott and Lou Costello seemed to pick up where Laurel and Hardy left off. The two worked together in vaudeville and radio and got their first break with 1940's *Night of*

Page 118: Shown here in 1929 in the two-reeleri *Liberty*, Stan Laurel and Oliver Hardy set a precedent for comic duos on the big screen.

Page 119: Actress Carole Lombard, the queen of the classic screwball comedy.

Opposite: The irrepressible comedy team of the Marx Brothers. From left: Chico, Groucho, Harpo, and Zeppo. As intelligent as he was funny, Groucho was a familiar sparring partner for the likes of Robert Benchley and Dorothy Parker at the Algonquin Hotel's legendary Round Table.

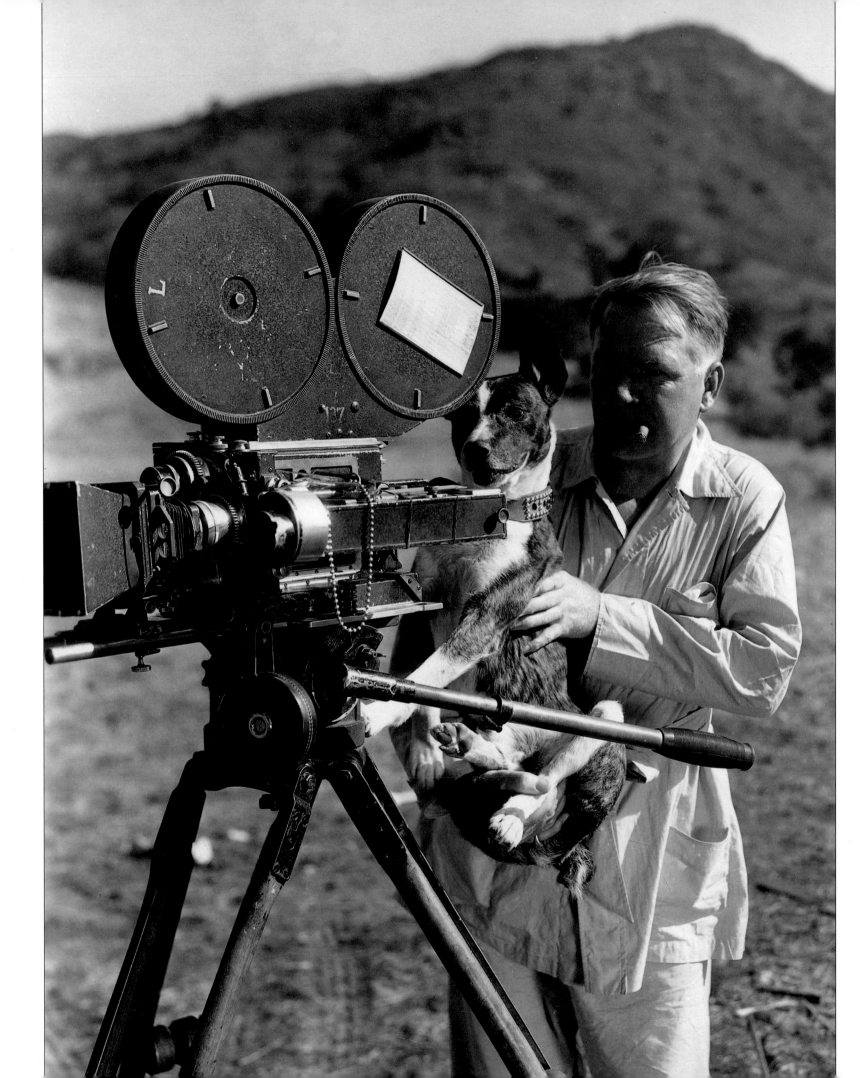

the *Tropics*, in which they delivered their ever-famous "Who's on First" skit. Throughout the 1940s and into the 1950s, Abbott and Costello turned out numerous films, including *Abbott and Costello in Hollywood* (1945), *Abbott and Costello Meet Frankenstein* (1948), *Abbott and Costello Meet the Invisible Man* (1951), *Abbott and Costello Meet Dr. Jekyll and Mr. Hyde* (1953), and *Abbott and Costello Meet the Mummy* (1955), among others. The duo broke up in 1956.

Just as Abbott and Costello took the reins from Laurel and Hardy, Dean Martin and Jerry Lewis—the handsome, crooning straight man and his goofy sidekick, respectively—seemed destined to resume where Bud and Lou left off. But the partnership was short-lived. The pair got a few chuckles with several films, such as *Living It Up* (1954) and *Artists and Models* (1955), before splitting up in 1956 to pursue separate careers.

Perfect Screwballs— and Then Some
....

W.C. Fields began his career in the silents, but really made a splash in the 1930s when he opened his mouth. Similar to both the Marx Brothers and Mae West in that he was a master of verbal comedy, he used the image of the eternal misanthrope to disarm audiences. He loved to hate everyone. When asked how he liked children, he answered, "parboiled."

While his comedy was a perfect foil for the day's straightlaced status quo, Fields eventually ran out of steam. But

when he was hot, he was hot. He costarred with some of Hollywood's biggest names, among them Burns and Allen, Bing Crosby, and Mae West. His best films included *It's a Gift* (1934), *The Man on the Flying Trapeze* (1935), *David Copperfield* (1935), *You Can't Cheat an Honest Man* (1939), and *My Little Chickadee* (1940). He died in 1945.

Carole Lombard was a darling of the silver screen, possessing a charm that translated well into both comedy and drama, but her talent for screwball comedies made her a star. Lombard made two films in the early 1930s with her real-life leading men: *Ladies' Man* (1931), with then-husband William Powell, and *Man of the World* (1932), with Clark Gable. Both marriages would be short-lived. Lombard divorced Powell in 1933 after only two years, and married Clark Gable in 1939—a union that would end tragically three years later.

Lombard's performance in *Twentieth Century* (1934), opposite John Barrymore, set the standard for the screwball comedy genre. For *My Man Godfrey* (1936), Lombard nailed an Oscar nomination—as did ex-husband William Powell. Several screwballs followed, including *True Confession* (1937) with Fred MacMurray. Lombard tiptoed into drama with mediocre films such as *Made for Each Other* (1939) and *In Name Only* (1939), but soon returned to the genre that best suited her, starring in *Mr. & Mrs. Smith* (1941),

Opposite: W.C. Field and friend behind the camera. Field's humor was strongly based on misanthropy and his lack of sobriety: "A woman drove me to drink and I never even had the courtesy to thank her."

Hitchcock's only turn at screwball comedy. Her last film, *To Be or Not to Be* (1942), was released shortly after her tragic death in a plane crash.

The former husband of the screwball goddess, William Powell first appeared—unfeatured—in *Sherlock Holmes* (1922). From there, his roles switched back and forth from sleuth to screwball, sometimes possessing a little of both. After finding career stability with *The Last Command* in 1928, he rose to stardom in 1929 playing the detective Philo Vance in *Canary Murder Case*, followed by *The Greene Murder Case* (1929), and *Benson Murder Case* (1930); he revived the role in 1933 in *The Kennel Murder Case*. In 1934, he appeared opposite rival Clark Gable in *Manhattan Melodrama*. Proving his screwball prowess, Powell was nominated for an Academy Award for his performance opposite Lombard in *My Man Godfrey* (1936).

Powell is perhaps best remembered for his *Thin Man* series with Myrna Loy. *The Thin Man* (1934) brought him another Oscar nod. Several more *Thin Man* films followed, some more successful than others. His onscreen chemistry with Loy led the duo to make a number of other films, including *I Love You Again* (1940) and *Love Crazy* (1941). Powell received another Oscar nomination for 1947's *Life with Father*.

The late 1940s and early 1950s brought Powell less stellar roles. He was delightful in *Mr. Peabody and the Mermaid* (1948), but he spent the rest of his career mostly in supporting roles, as in *The Girl Who Had Everything* (1953), *How to Marry a Millionaire* (1953), and his final film, *Mister Roberts* (1955).

Myrna Loy enjoyed a considerable career of her own. Her earliest roles, during the transitional silent-to-sound period of the late 1920s, were mostly dramatic. Then a high-spirited role in 1933's *Penthouse* brought her important recognition and the opportunity of a lifetime—the chance to play Nora Charles in the *Thin Man* series. The late 1930s would mark the apex of her stardom. She was named "queen of Hollywood" to Clark Gable's king.

Throughout the 1930s, Loy enjoyed huge success with both comedic and dramatic roles in such films as *Manhattan Melodrama* (1934), *Wife vs. Secretary* (1936), *Man-Proof* (1938), and *Lucky Night* (1939). She took a break from Hollywood during World War II to devote time to the war effort. When she returned in 1946, she did so stunningly with a role in *The Best Years of Our Lives*. More drama and come-dy followed in the 1940s and 1950s, including *The Bachelor and the Bobby-Soxer* (1947), with Cary Grant and a nearly full-grown Shirley Temple; *Mr. Blandings Builds His Dream House* (1948), also opposite Grant; and *The Ambassador's Daughter* (1956). In one of her final performances, she played Burt Reynolds's mother in *The End* (1978).

Left: Carole Lombard and William Powell were already divorced when they made *My Man Godfrey* (1936). Their onscreen chemistry, however, did not suffer one bit.

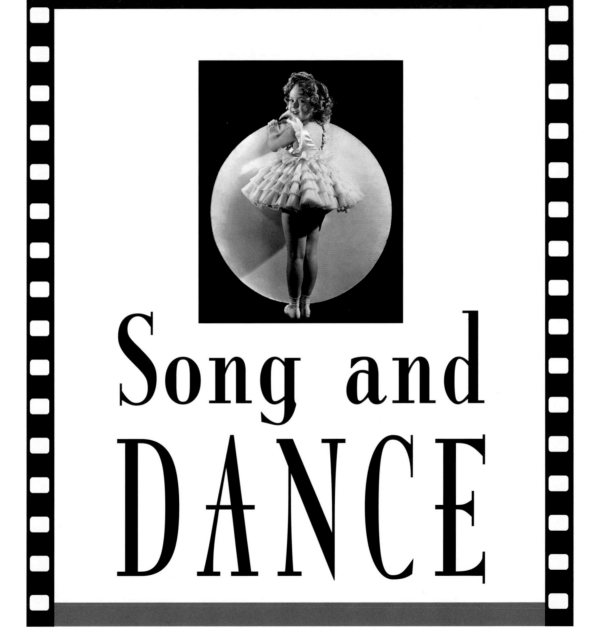

Song and
DANCE

They Danced on Air

Director Busby Berkeley achieved prominence during the 1930s with musicals that showcased Ziegfeld-type dancing girls and beautiful melodies. The "shows" always took place on a stage but in reality, no stage was ever large enough to contain Berkeley's flights of fancy. Curtains and sweeping staircases gave way to even more platforms and sets in ever-widening scope with hundreds of dancers performing precision-timed choreography, often shot from above and made to look like a living kaleidoscope.

Berkeley's female subjects were scantily clad and their virtues questionable. Moreover, the plot lines barely moved from point A to point B. However, *Gold Diggers of 1933* (1933) is a fine example of the dancing-girl choreography that became the Berkeley trademark; he repeated this prototype when he directed *Gold Diggers of 1935* (1935). Berkeley's work sparked the craze that became the Hollywood musical, and this genre brought its own dazzling brand of stars who swept down the aisles and into our hearts.

Rita Hayworth started dancing at twelve and was working in Hollywood nightclubs at seventeen. She was discovered by a Fox executive at one such location and rewarded with a role in *Under the Pampas Moon* (1935). She quickly earned a reputation as a hardworking and dedicated actress, and soon found her way to the A circuit.

First playing supporting roles to the likes of Joan Crawford in films like *Susan and God* (1940), Hayworth received great reviews, and ultimately her own starring roles—Fred Astaire handpicked her to be his costar in a couple of musicals, *You'll Never Get Rich* (1941) and *You Were Never Lovelier* (1942). While Hayworth was getting her first taste of stardom, she divorced Edward Judson to marry Victor Mature. When that engagement was broken, she married Orson Welles in 1944.

The 1940s proved magical for Hayworth. In 1946 fans lined the block repeatedly to see her move seductively in *Gilda*. Soon after, she took a step in another direction with *The Lady From Shanghai* (1948), written and directed by her now-ex-husband Welles, who starred in the film as well. One of the world's most desirable women, Hayworth created a publicity frenzy when she began a world-class courtship with international playboy Prince Aly Kahn, whom she married in 1949. She was once again divorced by 1951, and returned to work in Hollywood. In 1953 audiences drooled once more when she lit up the screen as the title character in *Miss Sadie Thompson*.

Page 126: Gene Kelly dancing on air in what is considered to be the best movie musical of all time, *Singin' in the Rain* (1952).

Page 127: Shirley Temple, shown here in her first film, *Baby Take A Bow* (1934), was instantly popular: by 1935 she was receiving 60,000 fan letters a month.

Opposite: Rita Hayworth singing "Put the Blame on Mame, Boys" in *Gilda* (1946). The success of her performance proved bittersweet: "Every man I've ever known has fallen in love with Gilda and wakened with me."

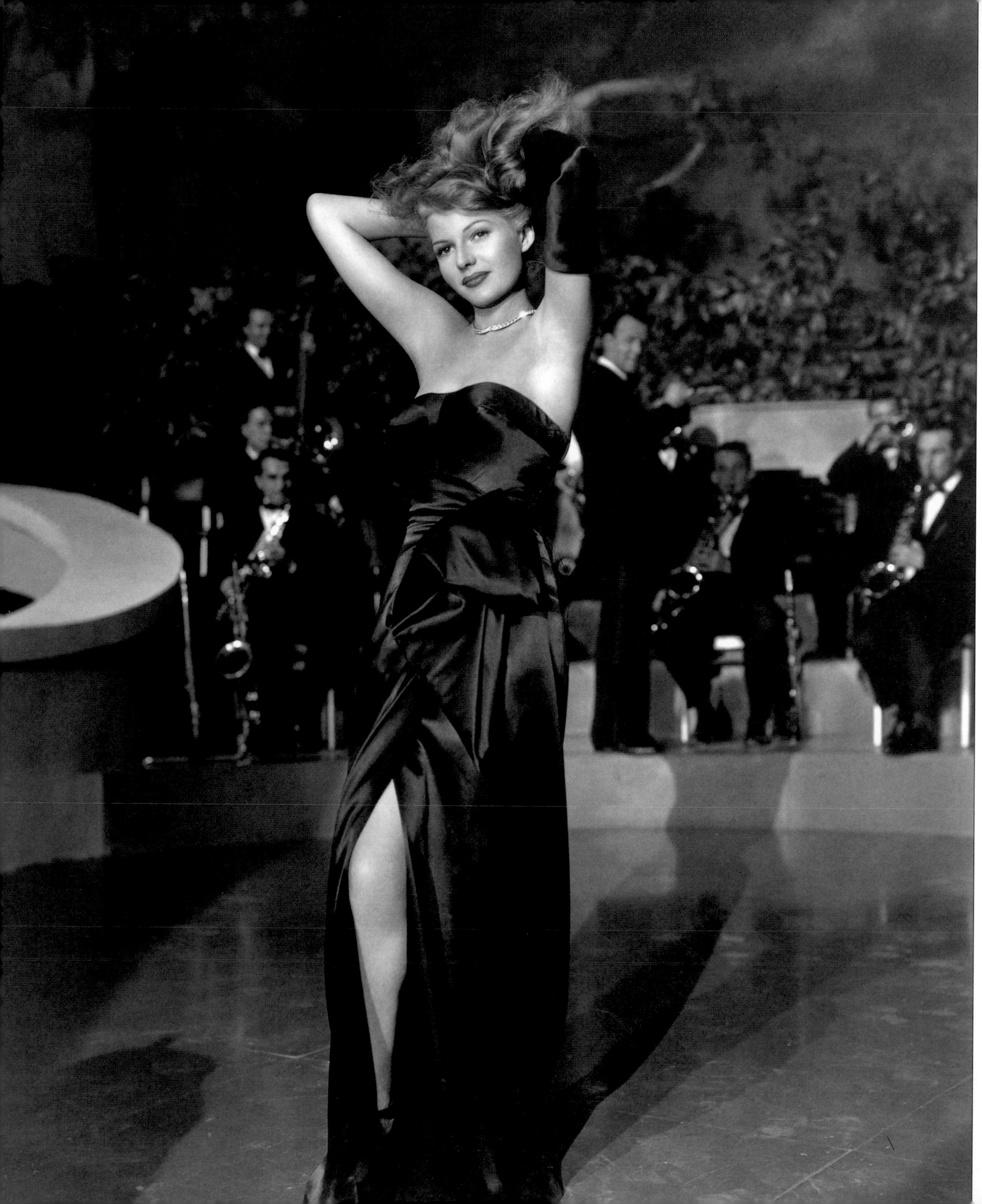

She spent her final years ravaged by Alzheimer's disease, dying in 1987.

Cyd Charisse started her career as a dancer. Born Tula Ellice Finklea, she changed her name in the early 1940s to Lily Norwood and made a rather inauspicious debut. When she arrived at MGM in 1946, she became—and remained—Cyd Charisse. It wasn't until Gene Kelly showcased her in two unforgettable dance routines in *Singin' in the Rain* (1952) that audiences sat up and took notice. The following year she appeared with Fred Astaire in *The Band Wagon*. Then she re-teamed with Kelly for *Brigadoon* in 1954. Another memorable success came in 1957, when Charisse and Astaire re-created the film *Ninotchka* in the Cole Porter musical *Silk Stockings*. The chemistry and grace of this partnership prompted critics to wonder whether it was Charisse and not Ginger Rogers who best matched Astaire's dance abilities. Charisse was sultry, sexy, leggy, and exquisitely talented.

Ginger Rogers made her first film, *Campus Sweethearts*, with Rudy Vallee in 1929. By then—at age eighteen—she was already a professional dancer, a vaudevillian, and a married woman. When she arrived in Hollywood, she got great breaks: *Professional Sweetheart* (1933), the musicals *Forty-Second Street* (1933) and *Goldiggers of 1933* (1933), and her

first film with partner Fred Astaire, *Flying Down to Rio* (1933). *The Gay Divorcee* (1934), *Top Hat* (1935), and *Shall We Dance* (1937) catapulted the pair to immortality.

When she wasn't gliding across the floor in the arms of Fred Astaire, Rogers tried her hand at drama, playing opposite Katharine Hepburn in *Stage Door* (1937). When her partnership with Astaire ended, Rogers's career was just beginning. In 1940 she gave an Academy Award-winning performance in *Kitty Foyle*, and went on in that decade to make a wide range of films, including comedies, musicals, and dramas.

Music Men
....

Dancer Fred Astaire, who had made an enormous impression on the public as far back as the 1930s with such partners as Eleanor Powell and Ginger Rogers, tried in vain to retire during the 1940s. By 1949, The Academy of Motion Pictures Arts and Sciences awarded him a special Oscar for his contribution to the American movie musical. Lured into various projects time and again, Astaire quietly continued to demonstrate his unique style and unmistakable elegance in dance and song well into the 1950s and beyond.

A star of the Broadway stage, Astaire had been performing with his sister Adele since 1917. When she retired in 1932, he decided to tackle Hollywood alone and wound up originating the art of the musical comedy. When he was first appraised by Hollywood bigwigs in 1933, the verdict was: "Can't act. Slightly bald. Can dance a little." Despite this lukewarm reception, he was featured in *Dancing Lady* (1933) and then paired with Ginger Rogers for *Flying Down to Rio* that same year.

Immensely charming and endearing, the slender Astaire was forever debonair and suave, fairly vibrating with internal rhythms. He referred to himself as a hoofer with a spare set of tails. Ballet choreographer Georges Ballanchine saw him a different way: "The greatest dancer in the world...You see a little of Astaire in everybody's dancing—a pause here, a move there. It was all Astaire originally."

After successful films with Rita Hayworth and Judy Garland, Astaire teamed up with Cyd Charisse, Oscar Levant, and Nanette Fabray for the four-star musical *The Band Wagon* (1953), then performed with Leslie Caron in *Daddy Long Legs* (1955), Audrey Hepburn in *Funny Face* (1957), and Cyd Charisse in *Silk Stockings* (1957). Irrepressible and irreplaceable, Astaire died in 1987 at the age of eighty-eight.

The talents of Danny Kaye, a Samuel Goldwyn star, shone in films tailor made to showcase his unique abilities. Starting off with *Up in Arms* (1944), Kaye mastered film acting, encompassing several genres: musicals, comedies, and dramas, including *The Secret Life of Walter Mitty* (1947), *The Inspector General* (1949), and *The Court Jester* (1956). He jammed with Louis Armstrong in *The Five Pennies* (1959) and played the Ragpicker in *The Madwoman of Chaillot* (1969). One of his most dramatic roles was in the television movie *Skokie* (1981), in which he played a concentration camp survivor. A great humanitarian, Kaye had a tremendous affinity for children and was one of UNICEF's first goodwill ambassadors.

Much more than a song-and-dance man, Gene Kelly got his start like most movie musical players—on Broadway. By the early 1940s, he had made it to Hollywood, starting out in *For Me and My Gal* (1942) with Judy Garland. Many more successful musicals followed, including *Cover Girl* with Rita Hayworth in 1944. In 1945, Kelly teamed up with director Stanley Donen and actor Frank Sinatra for the first time to make *Anchors Aweigh*, for which he won an Oscar. A pairing with Fred Astaire in *Ziegfeld Follies* (1946) followed.

Kelly reunited with Judy Garland for 1948's *The Pirate*, then Kelly and Sinatra found more success with *Take Me Out to the Ball Game* (1949) and *On the Town* (1949). *An American in Paris* (1951) earned him a special Academy Award. For Kelly, this movie was just the latest in a string of hits leading to a dazzling crescendo with *Singin' in the Rain* (1952), in which he starred and codirected with Stanley Donen. Kelly was Hollywood's roguishly handsome athletic dancer—innovative, gifted, and powerful.

Although he made several serious, dramatic films during his Hollywood career, Frank Sinatra is perhaps best remembered as the Voice, and when this voice made it to the movies, it sold tickets in large numbers. Sinatra first appeared onscreen in 1941 with the Tommy Dorsey band in *Las Vegas Nights*. *Higher and Higher* followed in 1943—giving Sinatra his first featured role. Later that decade, he sang and

Opposite: Judy Garland and James Mason in *A Star is Born* (1954). Friends and critics alike believed that Garland was a shoe-in for an Academy Award, but it was Grace Kelly who would take home the statue that year.

Hollywood's Brightest Stars

danced with Gene Kelly in *Anchors Aweigh* (1945), *Take Me Out to the Ball Game* (1949), and *On the Town* (1949).

Throat problems, bad publicity, and despondency over his failed marriage to Ava Gardner almost ended his professional career in the early 1950s. But when he read the part of Maggio in James Jones' book *From Here To Eternity*, he knew he had to play it onscreen. The studio finally gave in. Director Fred Zinnemann's *From Here to Eternity* (1953) won eight Oscars, including one for Sinatra, who had finally made a "comeback." Another nomination followed for his role as a junkie in *The Man With the Golden Arm* (1955). Back to musicals in 1955, he played opposite Marlon Brando in *Guys and Dolls*; reprised Jimmy Stewart's role in the remake of *The Philadelphia Story*, which was entitled *High Society* (1956); and crooned to perfection in *Pal Joey* (1957).

Sinatra continued to make powerful dramatic films through most of the 1960s. The tensely wrought and brilliant *Manchurian Candidate* (1962), however, was pulled from circulation after the assassination of President John F. Kennedy and not rereleased until 1987. Meanwhile, Sinatra and the Rat Pack, which included Shirley MacLaine, Dean Martin, Sammy Davis, Jr., Peter Lawford, and Joey Bishop, put out a few films, including the successful *Oceans Eleven* (1960), and *Robin and the Seven Hoods* in 1964. A powerful World War II adventure drama, *Von Ryan's Express* (1965) also received critical acclaim. *Tony Rome* (1967) and its sequel, *Lady In Cement* (1968), received a lukewarm reception. From then on, Sinatra placed more emphasis on worldwide concert appearances.

Divas
·············

Shirley Temple began her career in movies at the age of three, some say taking over where Mary Pickford left off. Temple was the youngest performer ever to receive an Academy Award. Darryl Zanuck signed Temple when he arrived at Fox, just in time to produce *The Littlest Rebel*. Zanuck saw the young girl's star potential and increased the budgets for her films and gave her stronger supporting casts.

Temple temporarily retired from films at age thirteen, but went back to them as a teenager with *The Bachelor and the Bobby-Soxer* (1947), among other less memorable films. She finally kissed Hollywood goodbye in 1949 at age twenty-one. In later years, Temple took her act on the road, so to speak, becoming active in politics.

Judy Garland enjoyed an illustrious career that unfortunately went awry when she became increasingly addicted to drugs and alcohol. However, her screen persona is immortal. She started out in *Broadway Melody of 1938* (1937) and subsequently teamed up with Mickey Rooney to make such musicals as *Babes in Arms* (1939) and *Girl Crazy* (1943). In 1939, she was cast as Dorothy in *The Wizard of Oz.*

Garland enjoyed several more musical successes: *For Me and My Gal* (1942), with Gene Kelly; *Meet Me in St. Louis* (1944); and *Easter Parade* (1948) among them. She was nominated for Academy Awards for *A Star Is Born* (1954) and for her dramatic performance in *Judgment at Nuremberg* (1961). Unfortunately, her personal demons got the best of her. She died of a drug overdose in 1969.

Although she is best remembered for her roles as Mary Poppins in 1964's movie of the same name and as Maria in *The Sound of Music* (1965), Julie Andrews has worked in many successful films, both musical and dramatic. In 1956, she starred in the television movie *High Tor* with Bing Crosby. Her dramatic appearances include roles in *The Americanization of Emily* (1964) and the 1966 Hitchcock film *Torn Curtain.* Andrews was nominated for Academy Awards for *The Sound of Music* and *Victor/Victoria* (1982), and she won for *Mary Poppins.*

Barbra Streisand made only sixteen films in the twentieth century. Not all of them are musicals, but they all carry the Streisand trademark—increasingly high budgets and a perfectionism that has made her more enemies than friends on the set. Streisand arrived on the Hollywood scene when she was barely twenty-one years old. Reprising her Broadway performance as Fanny Brice for the movie version of *Funny Girl* (1968) won her an Academy Award and worldwide recognition. Her next film, *Hello, Dolly!* (1969), was not as well received. Streisand's performance was nearly flawless, but she butted heads with director Gene Kelly and costar Walter Matthau more than once. From then on Streisand was known to be a difficult diva.

Streisand broke away from musicals and moved into comedy and drama for her next few films, including *The Owl and The Pussycat* (1970), with George Segal; *What's Up, Doc?* (1972), with Ryan O'Neal; and *The Way We Were* (1973), costarring Robert Redford. Streisand sang themes for many of her films, and shared the musical spotlight with Kris Kristofferson in the third reincarnation of *A Star Is Born* (1976). That effort brought her a co-Oscar win with composer Paul Williams for the song "Evergreen." The musical *Yentl* (1983), was the culmination of a ten-year labor for Streisand, who not only starred in it—she cowrote, produced, and directed as well. Despite the film's achievements, it was all but ignored by the Academy. Undaunted, Streisand has continued along the same path with such films as *The Prince of Tides* (1991), and *The Mirror Has Two Faces* (1996).

Opposite: Julie Andrews strumming between takes on the set of *The Sound of Music* (1965). Co-star Christopher Plummer observed: "Working with her is like being hit over the head with a valentine." Andrews has had similar feelings: "Sometimes I'm so sweet, even I can't stand it."

CHAPTER THREE

UNFORGETTABLE FILMS

On the evening of October 6, 1927, the first sound movie, *The Jazz Singer*, had a splashy Broadway premiere and changed the course of motion pictures history. There was much consternation that night. With the exception of the Warner brothers, the majority of studio czars had dismissed "talkies" as an expensive fad not worth consideration. But here was the pure voice of crooner Al Jolson flooding audiences with excitement. The studios quickly understood their grave miscalculation. The talkies were about to shake up Hollywood.

As the moguls faced the harrowing task of putting sound together with images, another problem emerged. With sound came language, some of it questionable, according to key ethical and political groups. They plotted to clean up Hollywood by forcing it to represent morals they deemed appropriate. Censorship was an anathema to filmmakers, so before a government crackdown could take place, Hollywood backers and principal players approached Presbyterian elder and postmaster general William H. Hays and asked him to become the president of a new organization, the Motion Pictures Producers and Distributors of America (MPPDA). By the 1930s, the Hollywood Production Code was put into place. Enforced by Joseph I. Breen, this agency was to grant an official seal of approval to all films that fell within established guidelines of moral decency. The Code put a halt to violence, sexual promiscuity, and off-color language. Even married sex was almost buried. One of the biggest laughs for future generations was the constant use of twin beds in married couples' bedrooms. The "Hollywood beds" lasted into the 1960s. In 1945, the MPPDA became the MPAA—the Motion Pictures Association of America.

Despite these and other hurdles—the arrival of television, the demise of the studio system, and the tendency toward higher and higher budgets, to name just a few—Hollywood has continued to thrive. The addition of color, new special effects, and enhanced sound has made the movies even more dazzling than ever. Public tastes have changed, and Hollywood has changed with them. And while those changes have sometimes meant the sad loss of the kinds of films that were once the rage (musicals, for examples, are no longer popular), they have also brought in fresh new voices, as more and more women and minorities have been able to tell their stories through film than ever before. Even as Hollywood has embraced the blockbuster, distribution arrangements between independent filmmakers and major studios have given films like *Clerks* (1994), *Fargo* (1996), *Pulp Fiction* (1994), and *The Brothers McMullen* (1995) an opportunity to shine.

As the business of movie making has grown and changed, so too have the films that Hollywood has produced. The pages that follow offer a glimpse at some of Hollywood's high points, the films which defined their genres or broke new ground. This is by no means an inclusive list of Hollywood's greatest achievements; it is, instead, a peek at some of the films that, at least in this authors' opinion, exemplify the magic of the movies.

Notable DRAMAS

Dramas have long been the mainstay of classical theater, so it is no surprise that Hollywood often looks to original plays and books for promising material. Marlon Brando became an international star screaming "Stell-uh!" while reprising his Broadway role of Stanley Kowalski in the screen version of the Tennessee Williams play *A Streetcar Named Desire* (1951). Surprisingly, the future Godfather did not win an Oscar for his performance, but both Vivien Leigh (as the unhinged Blanche Dubois) and Kim Hunter (as Kowalski's unfortunate wife) took home statuettes. Brando didn't have to wait long, however. In 1955, both he and Eva Marie Saint were rewarded for their work in *On the Waterfront* (1954), a compelling look at corruption in New York City harbor unions. The film brought in a total of eight Oscars, including Best Picture and Best Director (Elia Kazan).

Page 136: From left: Dooley Wilson, Humphrey Bogart, and Ingrid Bergman in *Casablanca* (1942), the film noir classic directed by Michael Curtiz.

Opposite: Montgomery Clift (left) and Frank Sinatra (right) in *From Here to Eternity* (1953) directed by Fred Zinnemann. Of Clift, director Edward Dmytryk quipped: "He was the most sensitive man I've ever known. If somebody kicked a dog a mile away, he'd feel it."

Although it's been remade more than once, the original *Mutiny on the Bounty* (1935), starring Charles Laughton, Clark Gable, and Franchot Tone, is by far the best version. This true British story of Fletcher Christian's mutiny against Captain Bligh won Best Picture honors. Another "water" film, this one taking place on an African river during WWI, is John Huston's *The African Queen* (1951). This movie provided Humphrey Bogart with his first and only Academy Award and earned Katharine Hepburn yet another nomination. Magic also exists in the stirring love story *Doctor Zhivago* (1965), which finds Omar Sharif cast as a Russian poet and doctor in love with a young nurse (Julie Christie) in a tragic saga about the Russian Revolution and its aftermath. The film won five Oscars. Another sweeping romance, *Wuthering Heights*, touched audiences in 1939.

Robert De Niro beefed up by gaining thirty pounds and won his first Oscar as boxer Jake La Motta in *Raging Bull* (1980). Another phenomenally successful boxing film, Sylvester Stallone's *Rocky* (1976), was the inspirational story of the 1970s. The movie ran away with Oscars for Best Picture and Best Director—and inspired four sequels.

Unforgettable
Films

Academy. Costar Frank Sinatra, however, was not. Diving into serious drama for the first time, he won a Best Supporting Actor Oscar. A total of eight Oscars went to this film, a sprawling soap opera based on James Jones's best-selling novel about U.S. Army life in Hawaii just prior to the Japanese attack on Pearl Harbor.

Jack Nicholson and Louise Fletcher both won Oscars for *One Flew Over the Cuckoo's Nest* (1975). Fletcher plays the tyrannical Nurse Ratched, while Nicholson is her nemesis and the champion of the inmates in an insane asylum.

Forrest Gump (1994) brought Winston Grooms's lovable character to the big screen. This tale of a simple-minded country boy who manages to become a war hero, millionaire, trendsetter, and father won the hearts of audiences everywhere, and captured six Oscars in the process, including Best Picture.

The everyman as a hero is, of course, not a new idea. Frank Capra moved people to laughter and tears with his singular vision that one ordinary person can make all the difference, in such classic films as *Mr. Smith Goes to Washington* (1939) and *It's a Wonderful Life* (1946), both starring Jimmy Stewart.

The Grapes of Wrath (1940), adapted from the novel by John Steinbeck, tells the story of migrant workers during the Depression. The film swept the Academy Awards, taking home Oscars for Best Actor (Henry Fonda) and Best Director (John Ford). The 1962 classic *To Kill a Mockingbird*, based on the novel by Harper Lee, examines racial politics from a child's point of view, and provided Gregory Peck with an Oscar for his portrayal of southern lawyer Atticus Finch.

A Place in the Sun (1951), starring Montgomery Clift, Shelley Winters, and Elizabeth Taylor, is based on Theodore Dreiser's *An American Tragedy*—a tale of a young man's fall from grace, brought on by the wealth and lifestyle he desires. The film won six Oscars, but the actors walked away empty-handed. Clift gave another memorable performance in *From Here to Eternity* (1953). But again, Clift was overlooked by the

Above: A pensive Gregory Peck as Atticus Finch in a scene from *To Kill a Mockingbird* (1962), directed by Robert Mulligan. The film marked the debut of Robert Duvall in the role of Boo Radley. To this day Peck stays in touch with his onscreen children, former child actors Mary Badham and Philip Alford.

Opposite: Laurence Olivier and Merle Oberon in *Wuthering Heights* (1939). Olivier was reluctant at first to accept the part of Heathcliff. Director William Wyler considered Robert Newton, but Samuel Goldwyn insisted on Olivier.

EPICS

Early on, producers learned that they could make a fortune at the box office by offering the public lavish spectacles based on grandiose themes. Spending the huge sums required was always a financial risk, but with the help of aggressive ad campaigns, producers had a better-than-average chance of earning back their investments tenfold. The legendary money makers speak for themselves, as do the failures, such as Michael Cimino's *Heaven's Gate* (1980), which brought down United Artists.

The Birth of a Nation (1915) was the first epic film. It depicts the evils of the Civil War and Reconstruction and traces their impact on two specific families. D.W. Griffith encountered heavy criticism for his depiction of the Klu Klux Klan as heroic, but the film is nonetheless accepted as a classic.

If ever there was a movie that captured the Civil War in the public imagination, it is David O. Selznick's 1939 masterpiece *Gone With the Wind*. Widely regarded as one of the greatest films ever made, this magnificent adaptation of Margaret Mitchell's novel demonstrates the strength of the human spirit through the character of Scarlett O'Hara, who refuses to accept defeat when the comfortable southern life she has always known crumbles around her.

Giant (1956), based on the novel by Edna Ferber, is the epic tale of two generations of Texans. With performances by Elizabeth Taylor, Rock Hudson, and James Dean (who was killed in a tragic accident shortly after the film wrapped), *Giant* became an instant classic and won two Oscars—one for George Stevens's direction, the other for Best Screenplay.

Ben-Hur (1959), directed by William Wyler, is perhaps the best of the numerous Bible epics made in the 1950s. A remake of the 1926 classic (which was in itself an epic, costing a then-unheard-of $4 million), it won a record eleven Academy Awards, including Best Picture, Director, and Actor. The film's incredible fifteen-minute chariot race and its depiction of galley slaves are more than worth the price of admission. A few years later, British director David Lean's *Lawrence of Arabia* (1962) brought the adventures of T. E. Lawrence to life on the big screen, winning seven Academy Awards and making an overnight star of actor Peter O'Toole.

Opposite: Charlton Heston rows for his life as a galley slave in a scene from the epic, *Ben-Hur* (1959).

In 1990, Kevin Costner made his directorial debut with *Dances With Wolves*, a saga (in which he also starred) about a Civil War soldier who befriends a Sioux Indian tribe. The film earned numerous Oscars including Best Picture, Director, and Screenplay.

It would be almost a decade before another epic film would fare as well. But in 1998, James Cameron's *Titanic* beat all the odds to become the most financially successful film of all time. The film focuses on the story of two fictional young lovers, played by teen idol Leonardo DiCaprio and Kate Winslet, aboard the doomed ship. Cameron's dedication to authenticity quickly added up to an unfathomable budget of $230 million, and when the film's release was delayed, many pundits guessed that the project would quickly go the

way of the ship. But despite bad reviews from notable critics, *Titanic* proved to be a phenomenal success, breaking all box-office records and bringing home eleven Oscars.

Above: Omar Sharif (left) and Peter O'Toole (center) in *Lawrence of Arabia* (1962). Contrary to popular belief, this was not O'Toole's debut. He had appeared in Disney's *Kidnapped* (1960) in a bagpipe duel with Peter Finch.

Opposite: Leslie Howard and Vivien Leigh in *Gone With the Wind* (1939) directed by Victor Fleming. David O. Selznick paid Margaret Mitchell $50,000 for the rights to her novel. Vivien Leigh earned $30,000. MGM loaned out Clark Gable, who did not want to make the picture, but a further Selznick bonus of $100,000 on signing sealed the deal.

Unforgettable
Films

Film NOIR

The film noir genre emerged during World War II, the by-product of two important developments in Hollywood. The first involved the technical way films were made during the war. Location shooting was next to impossible, rationing was on, and film budgets were curtailed. Access to certain raw materials necessary for glossy filmmaking was limited. A second influence came from a new breed of writers and directors who brought to their movies a European sensibility, much of it derived from German fatalism. Their films expressed the world-weary bleakness they had experienced before arriving in Hollywood.

Apart from sharing similar production aspects, such as shadows, fog, backlighting, bare bulbs, gloom, dark alleys, and dim interiors, films noirs tell stories of claustrophobia, isolation, and alienation and present bleak psychological landscapes. They envelop the audience in a cocoon of danger, suspense, intrigue, secret thrills, and hot passion. The French, upon seeing these movies after the war, dubbed them

Opposite: Orson Welles (left) and Joseph Cotten (right) in *Citizen Kane* (1941). Welles handled every aspect of the film—writing, producing, acting, directing, and overseeing set decoration and sound.

films noirs, a reference to American crime novels by such authors as Mickey Spillane, Dashiell Hammett, and Raymond Chandler, which were printed with black covers in France.

Noir giant *Citizen Kane* (1941), the American Film Institute's number-one film of the twentieth century, was Orson Welles's first effort, and undeniably his best. The controversial film is a fictionalized account of the life of newspaper magnate William Randolph Hearst, who tried to block the film's release after he heard about its content. Because of Hearst's highly visible protests and power, the film arrived at its premiere wrapped in a veil of unprecedented sensationalism.

With Humphrey Bogart's work in *The Maltese Falcon* (1941) and *Casablanca* (1942), viewers find a likable rogue, a tough hero who, for all intents and purposes, is ethical. *Casablanca*, probably the most romantic movie in the film noir genre, serves up a remarkable musical score, exotic locales, and a bittersweet love story. It took the Oscar for Best Picture and became a Bogart-cult classic.

All About Eve (1950) depicts the downfall of a Broadway star (played by Bette Davis) at the hands of a conniving, rising ingenue (Anne Baxter). It goes on to hint at the same

Another dark examination of the movies, Billy Wilder's *Sunset Blvd.*, was given a splashy premiere at Radio City Music Hall on August 10, 1950. A biting black comedy filled with insight into the studio system at the height of its powers, the film tells the story of an aging silent-screen star, Norma Desmond (played by Gloria Swanson), who lives like a Dickensian Miss Havisham within the walls of stopped time. The film earned high honors, but at a private industry screening in Hollywood, Louis B. Mayer flew into a characteristic rage and shouted at Billy Wilder: "You bastard, you have disgraced the industry that made you and fed you. You should be tarred and feathered and run out of Hollywood."

Director Roman Polanski resurrected the noir tradition in 1974 with *Chinatown*. This tale features Jack Nicholson as detective Jake Gittes, who chases femme fatale Faye Dunaway through a complex web of corruption and violence in 1930s Los Angeles. Polanski appears in cameo in the film, while legendary director John Huston plays a formidable villain. The film raked in Oscar nominations for Best Picture, Director, Actor, Actress, and a host of other awards, but only nabbed one statuette, for Robert Towne's screenplay. A sequel, *The Two Jakes* (1990), was disappointing, but the genre was revived to rave reviews with *L.A. Confidential* (1997), a hard-boiled police drama featuring Kevin Spacey, Russell Crowe, and Kim Basinger. The film earned nine nominations and took home two Oscars for Best Original Screenplay and Best Supporting Actress (Basinger).

fall from grace engineered by yet another fresh face once the ingenue is crowned queen. This dark and moody film is a scathingly witty look at the world of theater and Hollywood. It took home six Oscars.

Above: Peter Lorre (left) and Humphrey Bogart in *The Maltese Falcon* (1941). The movie is a classic "film noir" archetype wherein the female lead (Mary Astor) is usually motivated by lust or greed and must be punished one way or another.

Opposite: Gloria Swanson slaps William Holden in *Sunset Blvd.* (1950). This black comedy provides biting insight into Hollywood at the apex of its power—and foretold the fall of mogul Louis B. Mayer.

THRILLERS, SUSPENSE, CRIME, AND HORROR

Hair-raising stories have excited audiences throughout history and Hollywood has provided an enormous number of immortal and horrifying moments on screen. Numerous directors, writers, and actors have made names for themselves under the umbrella of this multi-faceted genre, from Orson Welles in the post–World War II classic *The Third Man* (1949) to Jodie Foster and Anthony Hopkins in the Academy Award–winning *The Silence of the Lambs* (1991).

It is almost impossible to examine movie suspense and horror without first considering the master, Alfred Hitchcock. His brand of horror has chilled audiences to the bone by suggesting that evil lurks everywhere—even in our own backyards. In *Rear Window* (1954), a murder unfolds in front of wheelchair-ridden Jimmy Stewart as he watches from his apartment window. In *Vertigo* (1958), Stewart returns, this time playing a retired detective hired to keep an eye on his friend's wife

(Kim Novak), on whom he develops a romantic fixation. *North by Northwest* (1959) transforms matinee idol Cary Grant into an action hero. Playing a Madison Avenue executive suspected of being a double agent, Grant's character is propelled into a nightmare of mistaken identity, police hunts, murder attempts, and a unforgettable game of hide-and-seek on Mount Rushmore.

Hitchcock redefined the horror genre in 1960 with *Psycho*. Full of surprises from start to finish, the film made audiences nervous about taking showers for a long time. Hitchcock spooked audiences once again with *The Birds* (1963), starring Tippi Hedren.

The success of Arthur Penn's *Bonnie and Clyde* (1967) spawned a wave of crime films in Hollywood. Starring Warren Beatty and Faye Dunaway, the film presents a stunning portrayal of the real life bank-robbing couple who terrorized the American Midwest in the 1930s. Its graphic violence and slow-motion sequences quickly established new trends in film technique and it won Oscars for Best Supporting Actress (Estelle Parsons), and Cinematography (Burnett Guffey). *The Wild Bunch* (1969), starring William Holden and Ernest Borgnine,

Opposite: Anthony Perkins in *Psycho* (1960). Perkins excelled at portraying troubled, lonely youths, often obsessed by older women, and easily crossed the line from "troubled" to psychopathic. In *Desire Under the Elms* (1958) he lusted after Sophia Loren, in *Goodbye Again* (1961) he wooed Ingrid Bergman, and in *Phaedra* (1962) pined for Melina Mercouri.

Unforgettable
Films

looks at aging outlaws eager for one last chance to raise hell.

Butch Cassidy and the Sundance Kid (1969) follows the true

adventures of two more American outlaws, played by Robert

Redford and Paul Newman. The film won four Oscars.

Francis Ford Coppola's *The Godfather* (1972) brought the

Mario Puzo novel to life in extraordinary detail. Its success

paved the way for an equally impressive sequel, *The*

Godfather Part II (1974). Moving brutality to deadlier heights,

Martin Scorsese's *Goodfellas* (1990) recounts one man's

attempt to become a Mafia wiseguy. Ray Liotta, Robert De

Niro, Paul Sorvino, and Joe Pesci (who won the Best

Supporting Actor Oscar) round out the cast.

Above: Warren Beatty and Faye Dunaway in a suggestive pose from
Bonnie and Clyde (1967). Beatty is fiercely private: "I'd rather ride down
the street on a camel than give...an in-depth interview. I'd rather ride
down the street on a camel nude. In a snowstorm. Backward."

Opposite: Francis Ford Coppola's brilliant *The Godfather* was a masterful
adaption of Mario Puzo's novel. The violent, sweeping epic, along with its
two unusually strong sequels, traces the history of a fictional Italian-
American crime family over three generations.

Hollywood Goes to War

War has always impacted Hollywood. In the past, stars have raised funds for war bonds, enlisted into armed service, made cross-country trips to rally support, or flown overseas to entertain troops, while filmmakers have increased audience awareness by creating powerful and provocative wartime films.

All Quiet on the Western Front (1930) was the first of the most memorable films of this genre. In its compelling depiction of the experience of young German soldiers in WWI, it opened audiences' eyes to the suffering people endure on both sides of a conflict. The film won Oscars for Best Picture and Best Director.

A winner of seven Oscars, *The Best Years of Our Lives* (1946), starring Frederic March and Myrna Loy, chronicles the lives of three veterans of World War II and how they cope after the war. *The Bridge on the River Kwai* (1957) follows the experience of British soldiers in a Japanese POW camp. William Holden and Alec Guinness were featured in this

Opposite: Robert De Niro (left) and John Savage (right) in *The Deer Hunter* (1978), a searing tale that examines the lives of Pennsylvania steelworkers before, during, and after the Vietnam War.

powerful drama that swept up seven Oscars. Also depicting the World War II era, *Patton* (1970) is a brilliant biography of the decorated general. In addition to winning Best Actor (George C. Scott) and Best Picture, *Patton* walked off with Best Director and Best Screenplay honors.

One of the most compelling dramas set in World War II is Steven Spielberg's *Schindler's List* (1993), which sheds a powerful light on the little-known life of Oskar Schindler, a Catholic war profiteer who abandoned a lucrative arrangement he'd worked out with the Nazis in order to save the lives of 1,000 Polish Jews, bankrupting himself in the process. Shot in a gloomy atmosphere of black-and-white, the film stars Liam Neeson as Oskar Schindler, Ben Kingsley as Schindler's accountant, and Ralph Fiennes as a Nazi commandant. *Schindler's List* earned seven Oscars, including Best Picture.

World War II went to the Oscars in numbers in 1998. Three films—Steven Spielberg's *Saving Private Ryan*, Terrence Malick's *The Thin Red Line*, and Roberto Benigni's *Life is Beautiful*—garnered Best Picture nominations. Spielberg and Malick's offerings are gut-wrenching depictions of the horrors of battle, while Benigni's sweet dramatic comedy focuses on a father's attempt to shelter his child from the horrors of a Nazi concentration camp. Spielberg took the Oscar for Best Direction and Benigni won for Best Actor and Best Foreign Film.

The Korean War is examined in a satirical light in Robert Altman's 1970 film *MASH*, starring Donald Sutherland, Elliott Gould, and Sally Kellerman. Despite the impressive performances of the cast, the film won only a single Oscar—Best Screenplay; however, it spawned a somewhat less mordant television series that played to large audiences for eleven seasons.

The horrors of Vietnam have been explored in numerous films, including *The Deer Hunter* (1978), with Robert De Niro and Meryl Streep (five Oscars); *Apocalypse Now* (1979), an updated version of Joseph Conrad's novel *Heart of Darkness*, starring Marlon Brando, Robert Duvall, and Martin Sheen; *Platoon* (1986), with Tom Berenger, Willem Dafoe, and Charlie Sheen, and *Coming Home* (1978). *Platoon* was based on director Oliver Stone's experience in Vietnam and won an Oscar for Best Picture. *Coming Home* took three Oscars, for Best Screenplay, Best Actress (Jane Fonda), and Best Actor (Jon Voight).

156

Unforgettable Films

Right: Ben Kingsley (center) in *Schindler's List* (1993). The film underwent numerous years of thought and pre-production before Spielberg felt ready to tackle it. Stamped with the director's characteristic frenzy, this true story of the Holocaust is a Spielberg masterpiece.

The Wild, Wild West

For years, the Old West was a mainstay of Hollywood production, and for two decades John Wayne sat tall in the saddle in a variety of westerns, often portraying a hero of the U.S. Cavalry. Most of these were directed by John Ford. But in the 1950s, another type of western emerged, the thinking-man's western, dealing with internal struggles of character rather than cowboys versus Indians.

Using a western backdrop for an allegory about modern-day America, Fred Zinnemann's *High Noon* (1952) is an assault on the cowardly majority, on its lack of will to stand up to a clearly defined enemy. The film stars Gary Cooper and Grace Kelly.

Equally impressive is George Stevens's *Shane* (1953) starring Alan Ladd, Jean Arthur, and Jack Palance. The film

Opposite: Gary Cooper won an Oscar for his performance in *High Noon* (1952), widely received as one of Hollywood's greatest westerns.

Above: John Wayne came to typify the all-American hero, embodying the righteous values of the mid twentieth-century. Though he made non-western films, he is most remembered sitting tall in the saddle.

examines the ideals that formed the grassroots beliefs of the United States and questions their virtues through portraits of corrupt and psychotic gunmen. *The Searchers* (1956) finds John Wayne as a man on a mission to rescue his niece (Natalie Wood) from Indian abductors.

In 1992, Clint Eastwood reincarnated the Hollywood western with an anti-western twist. *Unforgiven*, directed by and starring Eastwood, examines the morality of the Old West. It earned four Oscars, including Best Picture, Director, and Supporting Actor (Gene Hackman).

Sci-fi, Fantasy, and ADVENTURE

Frankenstein (1931) started the monster-movie trend, featuring Boris Karloff as the creature created by the mad scientist in Mary Shelley's novel. The film made Karloff a star. And the monster movies kept coming. While undergoing an apprenticeship of sorts at RKO, David O. Selznick produced *King Kong* (1933). Audiences marveled at the special effects as the gorilla trampled his way to the top of the newly built Empire State Building.

The science fiction movie *2001: A Space Odyssey* (1968) exposed another kind of monster that humankind could create, if it were not careful—that of the computer. Directed by Stanley Kubrick, the film received Oscar nominations for Best Director and Best Screenplay. Kubrick received a special visual effects Oscar for his work.

If the horror of *Jaws* (1975) started Steven Spielberg's career in earnest, then it was science fiction that made him

Opposite: Stephen Spielberg's *E.T. The Extra-Terrestrial* (1982) taps into the wonder of a child's heart. Filled with innocence and warmth, the film's mass appeal made it a blockbuster hit that reaped both high critical praise and awards.

a household name. For his next two films, *Close Encounters of the Third Kind* (1977) and *E.T. The Extra-Terrestrial* (1982), Spielberg brought the wonder of other worlds to earth, and created a box-office effect known as the blockbuster. Continuing the trend, George Lucas' *Star Wars* (1977) pushed an old-style epic into outer space, with ground-breaking special effects, earning record amounts. Two sequels (*The Empire Strikes Back*, 1980, and *Return of the Jedi*, 1983) secured the trilogy's place in movie history. More than twenty years after the start of the *Star Wars* phenomenon, George Lucas released a fourth installment, *Episode I: The Phantom Menace* (1999), which is actually a prequel to the entire odyssey, tracing the early days of Obi Wan Kenobi and Darth Vader. Lucas and Spielberg teamed up in 1981 for *Raiders of the Lost Ark* (1981), which cast *Star Wars*' Harrison Ford as the swashbuckling Indiana Jones, dedicated to preserving precious artifacts. An action-adventure packed with dazzling effects, fantastic stunts, and nasty Nazis, the film spawned its own pair of successful sequels.

Unforgettable
Films

A SHOCK to the System

Over the years, many filmmakers have challenged the status quo with films dealing with unfamiliar or taboo issues, or broke ground in terms of the way the stories were told. Some of these revolutionary movies became classics. As they blazed trails with tales of rebellion, violence, and social conflict, entirely new genres arose in their wake.

A momentous film of youth, despair, and rebellion is found in *Rebel Without A Cause* (1955), starring James Dean, Natalie Wood, and Sal Mineo—all of whom met violent and unnatural deaths in real life. *Rebel* is the story of a small town, its bullies, and its hero worshipers. Violent and psychologically disturbing, the film remains powerful today as it addresses common issues of alienation, poor self-esteem, and the communication breakdown between parents and teens.

Other conflicts in the relationships between parents and children lie in *Guess Who's Coming to Dinner* (1967), which forces audiences to ask themselves how they feel about

interracial marriages. Spencer Tracy gave a powerful (and final) performance, as did Katherine Hepburn, who won yet another Academy Award. Rounding out the cast are Sidney Poitier and Katharine Hepburn's real-life niece, Katharine Houghton.

Easy Rider (1969) challenged the establishment by setting two bikers, (Dennis Hopper, who also directed, and Peter Fonda) on a cross-country trek with a drunken lawyer (Jack Nicholson) in tow. *Midnight Cowboy* (1969) looks at what happens to a small-town boy (Jon Voight) when he hits the big city and falls in with a street hustler (Dustin Hoffman). The film, which received three Oscars, was given an X rating for exploring the seamy side of New York City and the taboo world of male prostitution.

Also distinguished for its X rating is *A Clockwork Orange* (1971), Stanley Kubrick's horror classic based on the Anthony Burgess novel. The story chronicles a young man's (Malcolm McDowell) nihilistic mayhem and the way the establishment fights back through equally disturbing brainwashing. No one who saw the film would ever hear "Singin' in the Rain" quite the same way again.

Opposite: Sidney Poitier (left), Spencer Tracy (center), and Katharine Hepburn (right) in *Guess Who's Coming to Dinner* (1967), directed by Stanley Kramer. Tracy's performance alone, as a parent whose liberal values are put to the test, is worth the price of admission.

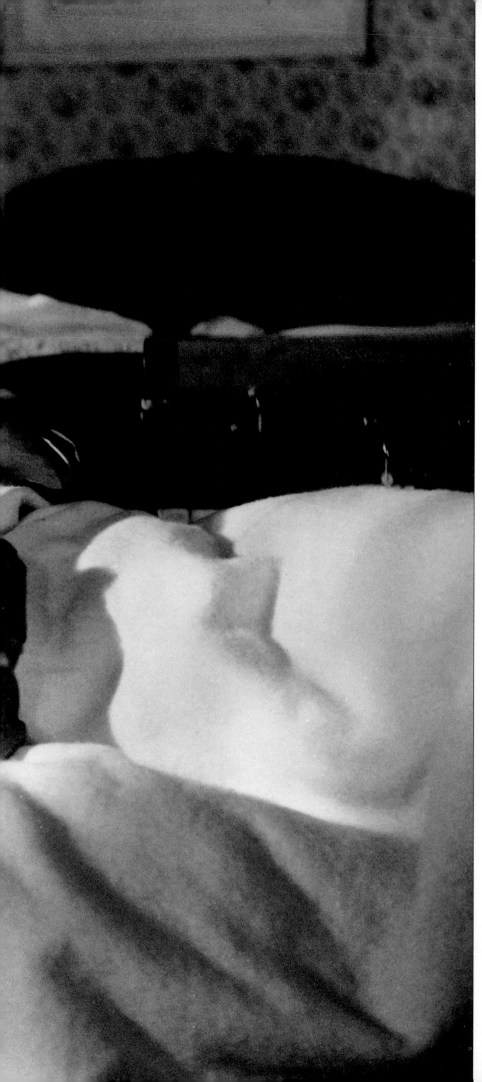

Martin Scorsese's *Taxi Driver* (1976), starring Robert De Niro, Cybill Shepherd, and Jodie Foster, is a depiction of a disturbed New York cabbie at a time when the city was experiencing urban decline. Its violence and depravity touched a highly sensitive nerve in audiences.

But almost twenty years later, after a steady stream of movie blood and guts, audiences were better equipped for Quentin Tarantino's sickly comedic *Pulp Fiction* (1994). Presenting intertwining stories, often difficult to piece together, the film looks at a pair of hit men (Oscar nominees John Travolta and Samuel L. Jackson) with a love of right-eous debate, a washed-out boxer (Bruce Willis) on the lam, whose plans hit a snag, and a drug lord (Ving Rhames) bent on revenge. Tarantino was nominated for Best Director, and he won the Oscar for Best Screenplay.

Left: Screenplay credit for Stanley Kubrick's film version of Vladimir Nabbokov's controversial *Lolita* (1962) was given to the author. But Nabokov's version (published later) is quite different from the final film.

Comedies

In the realm of silent films, nobody gave the world more humor or pathos than Charlie Chaplin. The laughter is endless in *The Gold Rush* (1925), and despite Chaplin's refusal to embrace the talking film revolution, he still amused brilliantly with *City Lights* (1931) and *Modern Times* (1936). The Marx Brothers continued the comedic dialogue with audiences—this time with words as well as sight gags—with the outrageously funny *Duck Soup* (1933), among others.

Screwball comedies emerged in the 1930s as a sub-genre of the romantic comedy in which curiosity and wit reign supreme. Wonderful to watch for their aesthetic values alone, these movies offer smart dialogue, endearing characters, and nonsensical stories that always prove logical in the end. The best among them, *It Happened One Night* (1934), *The Philadelphia Story* (1940), and *My Man Godfrey* (1936) pit rich against poor and give us a sense of how Depression audiences escaped the meanness of their daily lives.

Opposite: Tony Curtis eludes the bad guys by dressing up as a woman and joining an all-girl band—featuring Marilyn Monroe—in the comedy classic *Some Like It Hot* (1959).

Satire has always been an effective medium through which filmmakers can poke fun or state a case—sometimes softly, often with a highly caustic touch. *Network* (1976) is a scathing indictment of television and *The Apartment* (1960) illustrates the pitfalls of climbing the corporate ladder through morally questionable means.

American Graffiti (1973), written and directed by George Lucas, sparked a nostalgia movement by reminding audiences what is was like to come of age in the era of drive-in movies. The film showcased a slew of unknowns who went on to stardom, including Harrison Ford, Richard Dreyfuss, and former child-star Ron Howard.

Annie Hall (1977), a brilliant and intellectual comedy, written and directed by Woody Allen, stars Allen and Diane Keaton in an honest examination of relationships—from initial attraction to disintegration. The film swept almost all the Oscars, including Best Picture, Best Screenplay, Best Director, and Best Actress. It was the first comedy to be so honored since *It Happened One Night* (1934).

Musicals

The first talking film was essentially a silent movie with words and music added. Nonetheless, *The Jazz Singer* (1927), starring Al Jolson, revolutionized the film industry. In the 1930s and 1940s, Busby Berkeley almost single-handedly invented the movie musical—but not all the best efforts were his. *The Wizard of Oz* (1939), directed by Victor Fleming, was a musical fantasy that introduced the famous children's book series by L. Frank Baum to the big screen and experimented with a motion-picture first—splitting the film into black-and-white for reality sequences and Technicolor for fantasy.

In 1942, tough-guy icon James Cagney enjoyed a splashy success as singer-songwriter George M. Cohan in *Yankee Doodle Dandy*. Shedding his mobster persona long enough for rousing song and dance numbers, he displayed the very talents that had brought him to Hollywood in the first place, and he took home an Oscar for his effort.

According to MGM's market research, musicals were the most popular form of movie entertainment in the 1940s and 1950s, reaching a peak of perfection that lasted to the mid-

Opposite: Gene Kelly, singin' and dancin' in the rain. Newcomer Debbie Reynolds recalled that Kelly was relentless in his maniacal pursuit of perfection.

1960s. The 1950s started brightly with director Vincente Minnelli's *An American In Paris* (1951), built around a George Gershwin score. It starred actor-dancer-director Gene Kelly and newcomer Leslie Caron. *Singin' in the Rain* followed in 1952, and Kelly's jubilant romp through the raindrops is perhaps his most memorable onscreen number.

Movie musicals continued to attract audiences well into the 1960s with such award-winning films as *West Side Story* (1961), starring Natalie Wood, and Richard Beymer; *My Fair Lady* (1964) with Audrey Hepburn and Rex Harrison; *The Sound of Music* (1965), starring Julie Andrews and Christopher Plummer; and *Funny Girl* (1968) starring Barbra Streisand and Omar Sharif.

From the very beginning, Walt Disney's animated classics have featured musical numbers. *Snow White and the Seven Dwarfs* (1937), Disney's first full-length animated film, and *Fantasia* (1940) fit right in with the countless musicals of Hollywood's Golden Age. As tastes, budgets and the studio system changed, musicals almost disappeared entirely, but Disney forged ahead. Such films as *Beauty and the Beast* (1991) and *The Lion King* (1994) were so triumphant, they changed the way musicals flow. Instead of Hollywood adapting films from

Broadway shows, now Broadway adapts Disney's musical films for the stage with great success.

In the latter part of the century, only a few musicals have achieved any degree of commercial success. In 1971, Norman Jewison directed *Fiddler on the Roof* , an adaptation of the Broadway musical based on a story by Sholem Aleichem. An adaptation of the Broadway musical *Grease* (1978) featured John Travolta and Olivia Newton-John, and in 1996, the operatic *Evita* was brought to life, with Madonna in the title role.

More recently, a film's soundtrack has assumed a prominent position, very often triggering nostalgia, as in *The Big Chill* (1983), which is filled with Motown classics. When *Harry Met Sally* (1989) provided crooner Harry Connick Jr. with universal exposure plus the opportunity to blend torch-song standbys

with the romance of New York City. *The Graduate* (1967) included original songs by Simon and Garfunkel that touched a nerve in young audiences. In 1984, *Amadeus*—not a musical so much as a film with a wonderful score about a musical genius—took home seven Academy Awards, including Best Actor (F. Murray Abraham) and Best Picture.

Above: Tom Hulce as Mozart in *Amadeus* (1984). While some purists may object to Peter Shaffer's take on the persona of Mozart, they have to concede brilliance in F. Murray Abraham's award-winning performance as court composer Salieri. Haunting cinematography is a perfect match for the maestro's magnificent music.

Conclusion

It's hard to believe that one hundred years have passed since audiences first enjoyed a peek at Edison's initial foray into motion pictures. During the course of that century, the film world has progressed through the stages of infancy, golden childhood, and turbulent adolescence, ultimately reaching a state of maturity. The place films hold in American history is unique, for as they developed from flickering experiments to extraordinary marvels, they reflected the very century in which the United States took full possession of its nationhood.

What began as pure entertainment soon developed into something far more powerful—a phenomenon quickly grasped by the founding moguls, who realized that film was not just a form of entertainment, but a shaper of mass consciousness.

Today, films are available on laser disc and videocassette. There are movies made especially for network television and for specialty channels. There is free and abundant access to foreign films and pornography. There are children's films and documentaries made expressly for video. One might suppose that all of these would detract from the popularity of the feature films shown in the theater, but such is not the case. Film festivals have never been busier, and Americans still reserve time for viewing feature releases in theaters, where they can take advantage of the incredible sound systems and the wide screens.

There is something magical about sitting in a darkened room, something about the energy of a hundred strangers coming together to share a new experience. In that place, for those hours, nothing else exists or matters. That is the power of film.

In recent decades, technologies such as IMAX have enabled filmmakers to extend the horizon of filmmaking by revolutionizing the way we see images. In the near future, we may become even closer to the worlds portrayed in films by participating in them through virtual reality. Regardless of the level of technological sophistication, though, the essence of a film boils down to the story and how it makes us feel.

So long as movies can touch us, uplift us, disturb us, and enlighten us, so long as there is a personal dialogue between the dream and the dreamer, there will always be movie magic.

Academy Award Winners

1927–28
Outstanding Picture: *Wings*
Best Actor: Emil Jannings, *The Last Command* and *The Way of All Flesh*
Best Actress: Janet Gaynor, *7th Heaven*, *Street Angel*, and *Sunrise*
Best Director, Dramatic Picture: Frank Borzage, *7th Heaven*

1928–29
Outstanding Picture: *The Broadway Melody*
Best Actor: Warner Baxter, *In Old Arizona*
Best Actress: Mary Pickford, *Coquette*
Best Director: Frank Lloyd, *The Divine Lady*

1929–30
Outstanding Picture: *All Quiet on the Western Front*
Best Actor: George Arliss, *Disraeli*
Best Actress: Norma Shearer, *The Divorcée*
Best Director: Lewis Milestone, *All Quiet on the Western Front*

1930–31
Outstanding Picture: *Cimarron*
Best Actor: Lionel Barrymore, *A Free Soul*
Best Actress: Marie Dressler, *Min and Bill*
Best Director: Norman Taurog, *Skippy*

1931–32
Outstanding Picture: *Grand Hotel*
Best Actor: Wallace Beery, *The Champ*
Best Actress: Helen Hayes, *The Sin of Madelon Claudet*
Best Director: Frank Borzage, *Bad Girl*

1932–1933
Outstanding Picture: *Cavalcade*
Best Actor: Charles Laughton, *The Private Life of Henry VIII*
Best Actress: Katharine Hepburn, *Morning Glory*
Best Director: Frank Lloyd, *Cavalcade*

1934
Outstanding Picture: *It Happened One Night*
Best Actor: Clark Gable, *It Happened One Night*
Best Actress: Claudette Colbert, *It Happened One Night*
Best Director: Frank Capra, *It Happened One Night*

1935
Outstanding Picture: *Mutiny on the Bounty*
Best Actor: Victor McLaglen, *The Informer*
Best Actress: Bette Davis, *Dangerous*
Best Director: John Ford, *The Informer*

1936
Outstanding Picture: *The Great Ziegfeld*
Best Actor: Paul Muni, *The Story of Louis Pasteur*
Best Actress: Luise Rainer, *The Great Ziegfeld*
Best Director: Frank Capra, *Mr. Deeds Goes to Town*
Best Supporting Actor: Walter Brennan, *Come and Get It*
Best Supporting Actress: Gale Sondergaard, *Anthony Adverse*

1937
Outstanding Picture: *The Life of Emile Zola*
Best Actor: Spencer Tracey, *Captains Courageous*
Best Actress: Luise Rainer, *The Good Earth*
Best Director: Leo McCarey, *The Awful Truth*
Best Supporting Actor: Joseph Schildkraut, *The Life of Emile Zola*
Best Supporting Actress: Alice Brady, *In Old Chicago*

1938
Outstanding Picture: *You Can't Take It with You*
Best Actor: Spencer Tracy, *Boys Town*
Best Actress: Bette Davis, *Jezebel*
Best Director: Frank Capra, *You Can't Take It with You*
Best Supporting Actor: Walter Brennan, *Kentucky*
Best Supporting Actress: Fay Bainter, *Jezebel*

1939
Outstanding Picture: *Gone With the Wind*
Best Actor: Robert Donat, *Goodbye, Mr. Chips*
Best Actress: Vivien Leigh, *Gone With the Wind*
Best Director: Victor Fleming, *Gone With the Wind*
Best Supporting Actor: Thomas Mitchell, *Stagecoach*
Best Supporting Actress: Hattie McDaniel, *Gone With the Wind*)

1940
Outstanding Picture: *Rebecca*
Best Actor: James Stewart, *The Philadelphia Story*
Best Actress: Ginger Rogers, *Kitty Foyle*
Best Director: John Ford, *The Grapes of Wrath*
Best Supporting Actor: Walter Brennan, *The Westerner*
Best Supporting Actress: Jane Darwell, *The Grapes of Wrath*

1941
Outstanding Motion Picture: *How Green Was My Valley*
Best Actor: Gary Cooper, *Sergeant York*
Best Actress: Joan Fontaine, *Suspicion*
Best Director: John Ford, *How Green Was My Valley*
Best Supporting Actor: Donald Crisp, *How Green Was My Valley*
Best Supporting Actress: Mary Astor, *The Great Lie*

1942
Outstanding Motion Picture: *Mrs. Miniver*
Best Actor: James Cagney, *Yankee Doodle Dandy*
Best Actress: Greer Garson, *Mrs. Miniver*
Best Director: William Wyler, *Mrs. Miniver*

Best Supporting Actor: Van Heflin, *Johnny Eager*
Best Supporting Actress: Teresa Wright, *Mrs. Miniver*

1943
Outstanding Motion Picture: *Casablanca*
Best Actor: Paul Lukas, *Watch on the Rhine*
Best Actress: Jennifer Jones, *The Song of Bernadette*
Best Director: Michael Curtiz, *Casablanca*
Best Supporting Actor: Charles Coburn, *The More the Merrier*
Best Supporting Actress: Katina Paxinou, *For Whom the Bell Tolls*

1944
Best Motion Picture: *Going My Way*
Best Actor: Bing Crosby, *Going My Way*
Best Actress: Ingrid Bergman, *Gaslight*
Best Director: Leo McCarey, *Going My Way*
Best Supporting Actor: Barry Fitzgerald, *Going My Way*
Best Supporting Actress: Ethel Barrymore, *None but the Lonely Heart*

1945
Best Motion Picture: *The Lost Weekend*
Best Actor: Ray Milland, *The Lost Weekend*
Best Actress: Joan Crawford, *Mildred Pierce*
Best Director: Billy Wilder, *The Lost Weekend*
Best Supporting Actor: James Dunn, *A Tree Grows in Brooklyn*
Best Supporting Actress: Anne Revere, *National Velvet*

1946
Best Motion Picture: *The Best Years of Our Lives*
Best Actor: Fredric March, *The Best Years of Our Lives*
Best Actress: Olivia de Havilland, *To Each His Own*
Best Director: William Wyler, *The Best Years of Our Lives*

Best Supporting Actor: Harold Russell, *The Best Years of Our Lives*
Best Supporting Actress: Anne Baxter, *The Razor's Edge*

1947
Best Motion Picture: *Gentleman's Agreement*
Best Actor: Ronald Colman, *A Double Life*
Best Actress: Loretta Young, *The Farmer's Daughter*
Best Director: Elia Kazan, *Gentleman's Agreement*
Best Supporting Actor: Edmund Gwenn, *Miracle on 34th Street*
Best Supporting Actress: Celeste Holm, *Gentleman's Agreement*

1948
Best Motion Picture: *Hamlet*
Best Actor: Laurence Olivier, *Hamlet*
Best Actress: Jane Wyman, *Johnny Belinda*
Best Director: John Huston, *The Treasure of the Sierra Madre*
Best Supporting Actor: Walter Huston, *The Treasure of the Sierra Madre*
Best Supporting Actress: Claire Trevor, *Key Largo*

1949
Best Motion Picture: *All the King's Men*
Best Actor: Broderick Crawford, *All the King's Men*
Best Actress: Olivia de Havilland, *The Heiress*
Best Director: Joseph L. Mankiewicz, *A Letter to Three Wives*
Best Supporting Actor: Dean Jagger, *Twelve O'Clock High*
Best Supporting Actress: Mercedes McCambridge, *All the King's Men*

1950
Best Motion Picture: *All About Eve*
Best Actor: José Ferrer, *Cyrano de Bergerac*
Best Actress: Judy Holliday, *Born Yesterday*
Best Director: Joseph L. Mankiewicz, *All About Eve*
Best Supporting Actor: George Sanders, *All About Eve*

Best Supporting Actress: Josephine Hull, *Harvey*

1951
Best Motion Picture: *An American in Paris*
Best Actor: Humphrey Bogart, *The African Queen*
Best Actress: Vivien Leigh, *A Streetcar Named Desire*
Best Director: George Stevens, *A Place in the Sun*
Best Supporting Actor: Karl Malden, *A Streetcar Named Desire*
Best Supporting Actress: Kim Hunter, *A Streetcar Named Desire*

1952
Best Motion Picture: *The Greatest Show on Earth*
Best Actor: Gary Cooper, *High Noon*
Best Actress: Shirley Booth, *Come Back, Little Sheba*
Best Director: John Ford, *The Quiet Man*
Best Supporting Actor: Anthony Quinn, *Viva Zapata!*
Best Supporting Actress: Gloria Grahame, *The Bad and the Beautiful*

1953
Best Motion Picture: *From Here to Eternity*
Best Actor: William Holden, *Stalag 17*
Best Actress: Audrey Hepburn, *Roman Holiday*
Best Director: Fred Zinnemann, *From Here to Eternity*
Best Supporting Actor: Frank Sinatra, *From Here to Eternity*
Best Supporting Actress: Donna Reed, *From Here to Eternity*

1954
Best Motion Picture: *On the Waterfront*
Best Actor: Marlon Brando, *On the Waterfront*
Best Actress: Grace Kelly, *The Country Girl*
Best Director: Elia Kazan, *On the Waterfront*
Best Supporting Actor: Edmond O'Brien, *The Barefoot Contessa*
Best Supporting Actress: Eva Maria Saint, *On the Waterfront*

1955
Best Motion Picture: *Marty*
Best Actor: Ernest Borgnine, *Marty*
Best Actress: Anna Magnani, *The Rose Tattoo*
Best Director: Delbert Mann, *Marty*
Best Supporting Actor: Jack Lemmon, *Mister Roberts*
Best Supporting Actress: Jo Van Fleet, *East of Eden*

1956
Best Motion Picture: *Around the World in 80 Days*
Best Actor: Yul Brynner, *The King and I*
Best Actress: Ingrid Bergman, *Anastasia*
Best Director: George Stevens, *Giant*
Best Supporting Actor: Anthony Quinn, *Lust for Life*
Best Supporting Actress: Dorthy Malone, *Written on the Wind*

1957
Best Motion Picture: *The Bridge on the River Kwai*
Best Actor: Alec Guinness, *The Bridge on the River Kwai*
Best Actress: Joanne Woodward, *The Three Faces of Eve*
Best Director: David Lean, *The Bridge on the River Kwai*
Best Supporting Actor: Red Buttons, *Sayonara*
Best Supporting Actress: Miyoshi Umeki, *Sayonara*

1958
Best Motion Picture: *Gigi*
Best Actor: David Niven, *Separate Tables*
Best Actress: Susan Hayward, *I Want to Live!*
Best Director: Vincente Minnelli, *Gigi*
Best Supporting Actor: Burl Ives, *The Big Country*
Best Supporting Actress: Wendy Hiller, *Separate Tables*

1959
Best Motion Picture: *Ben-Hur*
Best Actor: Charlton Heston, *Ben-Hur*
Best Actress: Simone Signoret, *Room at the Top*
Best Director: William Wyler, *Ben-Hur*

Best Supporting Actor: Hugh Griffith, *Ben-Hur*
Best Supporting Actress: Shelley Winters, *The Diary of Anne Frank*

1960
Best Motion Picture: *The Apartment*
Best Actor: Burt Lancaster, *Elmer Gantry*
Best Actress: Elizabeth Taylor, *Butterfield 8*
Best Director: Billy Wilder, *The Apartment*
Best Supporting Actor: Peter Ustinov, *Spartacus*
Best Supporting Actress: Shirley Jones, *Elmer Gantry*

1961
Best Motion Picture: *West Side Story*
Best Actor: Maximilian Schell, *Judgment at Nuremberg*
Best Actress: Sophia Loren, *Two Women*
Best Director: Robert Wise/Jerome Robbins, *West Side Story*
Best Supporting Actor: George Chakiris, *West Side Story*
Best Supporting Actress: Rita Moreno, *West Side Story*

1962
Best Motion Picture: *Lawrence of Arabia*
Best Actor: Gregory Peck, *To Kill a Mockingbird*
Best Actress: Anne Bancroft, *The Miracle Worker*
Best Director: David Lean, *Lawrence of Arabia*
Best Supporting Actor: Ed Begley, *Sweet Bird of Youth*
Best Supporting Actress: Patty Duke, *The Miracle Worker*

1963
Best Motion Picture: *Tom Jones*
Best Actor: Sidney Poitier, *Lilies of the Field*
Best Actress: Patricia Neal, *Hud*
Best Director: Tony Richardson, *Tom Jones*
Best Supporting Actor: Melvyn Douglas, *Hud*
Best Supporting Actress: Margaret Rutherford, *The V.I.P.s*

1964
Best Motion Picture: *My Fair Lady*
Best Actor: Rex Harrison, *My Fair Lady*
Best Actress: Julie Andrews, *Mary Poppins*
Best Director: George Cukor, *My Fair Lady*
Best Supporting Actor: Peter Ustinov, *Topkapi*
Best Supporting Actress: Lila Kedrova, *Zorba the Greek*

1965
Best Motion Picture: *The Sound of Music*
Best Actor: Lee Marvin, *Cat Ballou*
Best Actress: Julie Christie, *Darling*
Best Director: Robert Wise, *The Sound of Music*
Best Supporting Actor: Martin Balsam, *A Thousand Clowns*
Best Supporting Actress: Shelley Winters, *A Patch of Blue*

1966
Best Motion Picture: *A Man for All Seasons*
Best Actor: Paul Scofield, *A Man for All Seasons*
Best Actress: Elizabeth Taylor, *Who's Afraid of Virginia Woolf?*
Best Director: Fred Zinnemann, *A Man for All Seasons*
Best Supporting Actor: Walter Matthau, *The Fortune Cookie*
Best Supporting Actress: Sandy Dennis, *Who's Afraid of Virginia Woolf?*

1967
Best Motion Picture: *In the Heat of the Night*
Best Actor: Rod Steiger, *In the Heat of the Night*
Best Actress: Katharine Hepburn, *Guess Who's Coming to Dinner?*
Best Director: Mike Nichols, *The Graduate*
Best Supporting Actor: George Kennedy, *Cool Hand Luke*
Best Supporting Actress: Estelle Parsons, *Bonnie and Clyde*

1968
Best Motion Picture: *Oliver!*
Best Actor: Cliff Robertson, *Charly*
Best Actress (tie): Katharine Hepburn, *The Lion in Winter;* Barbra Streisand, *Funny Girl*
Best Director: Carol Reed, *Oliver!*
Best Supporting Actor: Jack Albertson, *The Subject Was Roses*
Best Supporting Actress: Ruth Gordon, *Rosemary's Baby*

1969
Best Motion Picture: *Midnight Cowboy*
Best Actor: John Wayne, *True Grit*
Best Actress: Maggie Smith, *The Prime of Miss Jean Brodie*
Best Director: John Schlesinger, *Midnight Cowboy*
Best Supporting Actor: Gig Young, *They Shoot Horses, Don't They?*
Best Supporting Actress: Goldie Hawn, *Cactus Flower*

1970
Best Motion Picture: *Patton*
Best Actor: George C. Scott, *Patton*
Best Actress: Glenda Jackson, *Women in Love*
Best Director: Franklin J. Schaffner, *Patton*
Best Supporting Actor: John Mills, *Ryan's Daughter*
Best Supporting Actress: Helen Hayes, *Airport*

1971
Best Motion Picture: *The French Connection*
Best Actor: Gene Hackman, *The French Connection*
Best Actress: Jane Fonda, *Klute*
Best Director: William Friedkin, *The French Connection*
Best Supporting Actor: Ben Johnson, *The Last Picture Show*
Best Supporting Actress: Cloris Leachman, *The Last Picture Show*

1972
Best Motion Picture: *The Godfather*
Best Actor: Marlon Brando, *The Godfather*
Best Actress: Liza Minelli, *Cabaret*
Best Director: Bob Fosse, *Cabaret*
Best Supporting Actor: Joel Grey, *Cabaret*
Best Supporting Actress: Eileen Heckart, *Butterflies Are Free*

1973
Best Motion Picture: *The Sting*
Best Actor: Jack Lemmon, *Save the Tiger*
Best Actress: Glenda Jackson, *A Touch of Class*
Best Director: George Roy Hill, *The Sting*
Best Supporting Actor: John Houseman, *The Paper Chase*
Best Supporting Actress: Tatum O'Neal, *Paper Moon*

1974
Best Motion Picture: *The Godfather, Part II*
Best Actor: Art Carney, *Harry and Tonto*
Best Actress: Ellen Burstyn, *Alice Doesn't Live Here Anymore*
Best Director: Francis Ford Coppola, *The Godfather, Part II*
Best Supporting Actor: Robert De Niro, *The Godfather, Part II*
Best Supporting Actress: Ingrid Bergman, *Murder on the Orient Express*

1975
Best Motion Picture: *One Flew Over the Cuckoo's Nest*
Best Actor: Jack Nicholson, *One Flew Over the Cuckoo's Nest*
Best Actress: Louise Flecther, *One Flew Over the Cuckoo's Nest*
Best Director: Milos Forman, *One Flew Over the Cuckoo's Nest*
Best Supporting Actor: George Burns, *The Sunshine Boys*
Best Supporting Actress: Lee Grant, *Shampoo*

1976
Best Motion Picture: *Rocky*
Best Actor: Peter Finch, *Network*
Best Actress: Faye Dunaway, *Network*
Best Director: John G. Avildsen, *Rocky*
Best Supporting Actor: Jason Robards, *All the President's Men*
Best Supporting Actress: Beatrice Straight, *Network*

1977
Best Motion Picture: *Annie Hall*
Best Actor: Richard Dreyfuss, *The Goodbye Girl*
Best Actress: Diane Keaton, *Annie Hall*
Best Director: Woody Allen, *Annie Hall*
Best Supporting Actor: Jason Robards, *Julia*

Best Supporting Actress: Vanessa Redgrave, *Julia*

1978
Best Motion Picture: *The Deer Hunter*
Best Actor: Jon Voight, *Coming Home*
Best Actress: Jane Fonda, *Coming Home*
Best Director: Michael Cimino, *The Deer Hunter*
Best Supporting Actor: Christopher Walken, *The Deer Hunter*
Best Supporting Actress: Maggie Smith, *California Suite*

1979
Best Motion Picture: *Kramer vs. Kramer*
Best Actor: Dustin Hoffman, *Kramer vs. Kramer*
Best Actress: Sally Field, *Norma Rae*
Best Director: Robert Benton, *Kramer vs. Kramer*
Best Supporting Actor: Melvyn Douglas, *Being There*
Best Supporting Actress: Meryl Streep, *Kramer vs. Kramer*

1980
Best Motion Picture: *Ordinary People*
Best Actor: Robert De Niro, *Raging Bull*
Best Actress: Sissy Spacek, *Coal Miner's Daughter*
Best Director: Robert Redford, *Ordinary People*
Best Supporting Actor: Timothy Hutton, *Ordinary People*
Best Supporting Actress: Mary Steenburgen, *Melvin and Howard*

1981
Best Motion Picture: *Chariots of Fire*
Best Actor: Henry Fonda, *On Golden Pond*
Best Actress: Katharine Hepburn, *On Golden Pond*
Best Director: Warren Beatty, *Reds*
Best Supporting Actor: John Gielgud, *Arthur*
Best Supporting Actress: Maureen Stapleton, *Reds*

1982
Best Motion Picture: *Gandhi*
Best Actor: Ben Kingsley, *Gandhi*
Best Actress: Meryl Streep, *Sophie's Choice*
Best Director: Richard Attenborough, *Gandhi*
Best Supporting Actor: Louis Gossett Jr., *An Officer and a Gentleman*
Best Supporting Actress: Jessica Lange, *Tootsie*

1983
Best Motion Picture: *Terms of Endearment*
Best Actor: Robert Duvall, *Tender Mercies*
Best Actress: Shirley MacLaine, *Terms of Endearment*
Best Director: James L. Brooks, *Terms of Endearment*
Best Supporting Actor: Jack Nicholson, *Terms of Endearment*
Best Supporting Actress: Linda Hunt, *The Year of Living Dangerously*

1984
Best Motion Picture: *Amadeus*
Best Actor: F. Murray Abraham, *Amadeus*
Best Actress: Sally Field, *Places in the Heart*
Best Director: Milos Forman, *Amadeus*
Best Supporting Actor: Haing S. Ngor, *The Killing Fields*
Best Supporting Actress: Peggy Ashcroft, *A Passage to India*

1985
Best Motion Picture: *Out of Africa*
Best Actor: William Hurt, *Kiss of the Spider Woman*
Best Actress: Geraldine Page, *The Trip to Bountiful*
Best Director: Sydney Pollack, *Out of Africa*
Best Supporting Actor: Don Ameche, *Cocoon*
Best Supporting Actress: Anjelica Huston, *Prizzi's Honor*

1986
Best Motion Picture: *Platoon*
Best Actor: Paul Newman, *The Color of Money*
Best Actress: Marlee Matlin, *Children of a Lesser God*
Best Director: Oliver Stone, *Platoon*
Best Supporting Actor: Michael Caine, *Hannah and Her Sisters*
Best Supporting Actress: Dianne Wiest, *Hannah and Her Sisters*

1987
Best Motion Picture: *The Last Emperor*
Best Actor: Michael Douglas, *Wall Street*
Best Actress: Cher, *Moonstruck*
Best Director: Bernardo Bertolucci, *The Last Emperor*
Best Supporting Actor: Sean Connery, *The Untouchables*
Best Supporting Actress: Olympia Dukakis, *Moonstruck*

1988
Best Motion Picture: *Rain Man*
Best Actor: Dustin Hoffman, *Rain Man*
Best Actress: Jodie Foster, *The Accused*
Best Director: Barry Levinson, *Rain Man*
Best Supporting Actor: Kevin Kline, *A Fish Called Wanda*
Best Supporting Actress: Geena Davis, *The Accidental Tourist*

1989
Best Motion Picture: *Driving Miss Daisy*
Best Actor: Daniel Day-Lewis, *My Left Foot*
Best Actress: Jessica Tandy, *Driving Miss Daisy*
Best Director: Oliver Stone, *Born on the Fourth of July*
Best Supporting Actor: Denzel Washington, *Glory*
Best Supporting Actress: Brenda Fricker, *My Left Foot*

1990
Best Motion Picture: *Dances with Wolves*
Best Actor: Jeremy Irons, *Reversal of Fortune*
Best Actress: Kathy Bates, *Misery*
Best Director: Kevin Costner, *Dances with Wolves*
Best Supporting Actor: Joe Pesci, *GoodFellas*
Best Supporting Actress: Whoopi Goldberg, *Ghost*

1991
Best Motion Picture: *The Silence of the Lambs*
Best Actor: Anthony Hopkins, *The Silence of the Lambs*
Best Actress: Jodie Foster, *The Silence of the Lambs*
Best Director: Jonathan Demme, *The Silence of the Lambs*
Best Supporting Actor: Jack Palance, *City Slickers*
Best Supporting Actress: Mercedes Ruehl, *The Fisher King*

1992
Best Motion Picture: *Unforgiven*
Best Actor: Al Pacino, *Scent of a Woman*
Best Actress: Emma Thompson, *Howards End*
Best Director: Clint Eastwood, *Unforgiven*
Best Supporting Actor: Gene Hackman, *Unforgiven*
Best Supporting Actress: Marisa Tomei, *My Cousin Vinny*

1993
Best Motion Picture: *Schindler's List*
Best Actor: Tom Hanks, *Philadelphia*
Best Actress: Holly Hunter, *The Piano*
Best Director: Steven Spielberg, *Schindler's List*
Best Supporting Actor: Tommy Lee Jones, *The Fugitive*
Best Supporting Actress: Anna Paquin, *The Piano*

1994
Best Motion Picture: *Forrest Gump*
Best Actor: Tom Hanks, *Forrest Gump*
Best Actress: Jessica Lange, *Blue Sky*
Best Director: Robert Zemeckis, *Forrest Gump*
Best Supporting Actor: Martin Landau, *Ed Wood*
Best Supporting Actress: Dianne Wiest, *Bullets Over Broadway*

1995
Best Motion Picture: *Braveheart*
Best Actor: Nicolas Cage, *Leaving Las Vegas*
Best Actress: Susan Sarandon, *Dead Man Walking*
Best Director: Mel Gibson, *Braveheart*
Best Supporting Actor: Kevin Spacey, *The Usual Suspects*
Best Supporting Actress: Mira Sorvino, *Mighty Aphrodite*

1996
Best Motion Picture: *The English Patient*
Best Actor: Geoffrey Rush, *Shine*
Best Actress: Frances McDormand, *Fargo*
Best Director: Anthony Minghella, *The English Patient*
Best Supporting Actor: Cuba Gooding Jr., *Jerry Maguire*
Best Supporting Actress: Juliette Binoche, *The English Patient*

1997
Best Motion Picture: *Titanic*
Best Actor: Jack Nicholson, *As Good As It Gets*
Best Actress: Helen Hunt, *As Good As It Gets*
Best Director: James Cameron, *Titanic*
Best Supporting Actor: Robin Williams, *Good Will Hunting*
Best Supporting Actress: Kim Basinger, *L.A. Confidential*

1998
Best Motion Picture: *Shakespeare In Love*
Best Actor: Roberto Benigni, *Life is Beautiful*
Best Actress: Gwyneth Paltrow, *Shakespeare In Love*
Best Director: Steven Speilberg, *Saving Private Ryan*
Best Supporting Actor: James Coburn, *Affliction*
Best Supporting Actress: Judi Dench, *Shakespeare in Love*

Index